Koehler, Jack H. 1936-
Upscale nine-ball (Condensed version)
1. Sport 2. Billiards 3. Pool (Game) I. Title

Published by:

SPORTOLOGY PUBLICATIONS
N2689 Spring Lane
Marinette, WI 54143

International Standard Book Number:
978-0-9622890-4-0 (paper)

Printed in the United States of America

All cover art and illustrations by author

UPSCALE
NINE-BALL
(CONDENSED VERSION)

BY
Jack H. Koehler

SPORTOLOGY
PUBLICATIONS
Marinette, WI

Jack H. Koehler

DEDICATION

This book is dedicated to
the pool players of the
world, those of the past,
present, and future.

CONTENTS

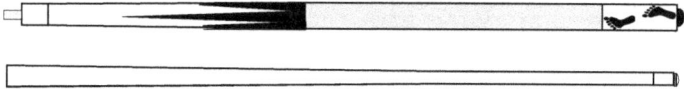

CONTENTS

UPSCALE NINE-BALL

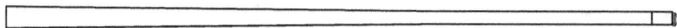

CHAPTER 1
INTRODUCTION

T his book is a condensed version of the original UPSCALE NINE-BALL book published in 2000. About 60 percent of the material that was in the original book has been left out of this book. After reading this book, if readers desire more in-depth information about NINE-BALL, it is suggested they read the original book.

It is difficult to write a book that will serve players of all skill levels. The novice player may consider some of the material too complicated and the skilled player may consider the same material too elementary. With this book it is assumed that the reader is familiar with the basics of pool, is accomplished in the game of EIGHT-BALL, and wants to move into the game of NINE-BALL.

Keep this in mind as a constant source of motivation: **"the moment you quit studying pool, your opponent is getting ahead of you."**

◆ ◆ ◆

1

EIGHT-BALL VERSES
NINE-BALL

Generally, most people learn to play the game of EIGHT-BALL before progressing to NINE-BALL. EIGHT-BALL is usually preferred by beginners because the rules are easy to learn and people can have fun playing even though they have no previous experience playing pool. To many, the socializing while playing EIGHT-BALL is more important than the game itself. The more serious EIGHT-BALL players may advance to playing in a league. Leagues typically consist of several bar teams (or other social groups) that compete against each other. A somewhat different innovation is the "in-house league" which consists of teams from a single establishment competing among themselves.

Whereas league play is the predominant forum for the serious EIGHT-BALL player, the **tournament** is the predominant forum for the serious NINE-BALL player. The tournaments are usually single or double elimination and emphasize individual against individual as opposed to team play. The underlying motivation for playing in NINE-BALL tournaments is competition rather than sociability.

Most EIGHT-BALL is played on what is called a "seven foot" or "barroom" table which is 40 inches wide and 80 inches long. If it is a coin-operated table, the cue ball may be heavier and sometimes larger than the object balls. Most serious NINE-BALL is played on "nine foot" or "regulation" tables, which are 50 inches wide and 100 inches long. When

2

playing on the larger tables the cue ball is generally the same size and weight as the other balls.

Old skills will have to be honed and new skills learned when making the transition from EIGHT-BALL to NINE-BALL. In NINE-BALL, because the table generally is larger, the shots are longer and thus require greater aiming accuracy. And, because there is only one object ball, the cue ball generally must be moved a greater distance in getting shape on the next ball. Consequently, positioning the cue ball requires greater skill in NINE-BALL.

Safeties are more prevalent and therefore more important in NINE-BALL. Kicking skills must be honed to help avoid fouling when responding to a safety. Also, english and shooting speed must be tuned to a finer degree because of more demanding cue-ball positioning requirements. Banking and kicking are more important in NINE-BALL and therefore should be studied and practiced more frequently. Because the cue ball must be moved farther between shots, the player must learn to use more cushions in getting shape. It is not unusual in NINE-BALL to have the cue-ball strike three cushions in getting to the desired position for the next shot.

The diversity of skills required by NINE-BALL players is evident when they play other pool games. Their dominance, even outside their specialty, can be partially explained by the fact that the *best* pool players in the world *must* play NINE-BALL if they want to make a living playing pool.

◆ ◆ ◆

RULES OF NINE-BALL

The general rules of pool apply to NINE-BALL. That is, at least one foot must be on the floor when shooting, etc. The following NINE-BALL rules were taken, verbatim, from *THE OFFICIAL RULES AND RECORDS BOOK* published by the Billiard Congress of America in 1999.

[World Standardized Rules]
Except when clearly contradicted by these additional rules, the **General rules of Pocket Billiards** apply.

5.1 OBJECT OF THE GAME. Nine Ball is played with nine object balls numbered one through nine and a cue ball. On each shot the first ball the cue ball contacts must be the lowest-numbered ball on the table, but the balls need not be pocketed in order. If a player pockets any ball on a legal shot, he remains at the table for another shot, and continues until missing, committing a foul, or wining the game by pocketing the 9-ball. After a miss, the incoming player must shoot from the position left by the previous player, but after any foul the incoming player may start with the cue ball anywhere on the table. Players are not required to call any shot. A match ends when one of the players has won the required number of games.

5.2. RACKING THE BALLS. The object balls are racked in a diamond shape, with the 1-ball at the top of the diamond and on the foot spot, the 9-ball in the center of the diamond, and the other balls in random order, racked as tightly as possible. The game begins with the cue ball in hand behind the head string.

Diamond Shaped Rack

1-ball must be on the foot spot.

9-ball must be in the center of the rack.

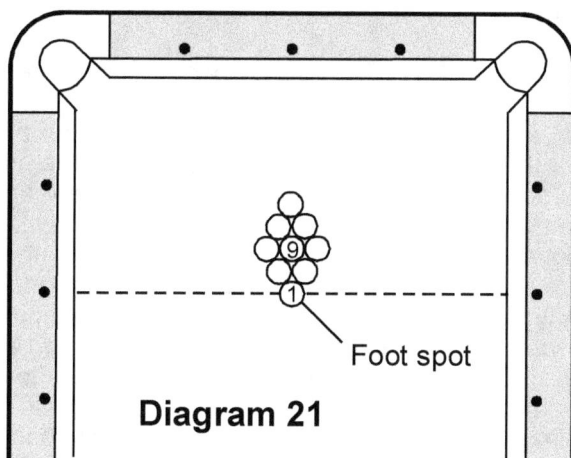

Foot spot

Diagram 21

5.3. LEGAL BREAK SHOT. The rules governing the break shot are the same as for other shots except:
1. The breaker must strike the 1-ball first and either pocket a ball or drive at least four numbered balls to the rail.
2. If the cue ball is pocketed or driven off the table, or the requirements of the opening break are not met, it is a foul, and the incoming player has cue ball in hand anywhere on the table.
3. If on the break shot, the breaker causes an object ball to jump off the table, it is a foul and the incoming player has cue ball in hand anywhere on the table. The object ball is not respotted (*exception: if the object ball is the 9-ball, it is respotted*).

5.4. CONTINUING PLAY. On the shot immediately following a legal break, the shooter may play a "push out." (*See rule 5.5*). If the breaker pockets one or more balls on a legal break, he continues to shoot until

5

he misses, fouls, or wins the game. If the player misses or fouls, the other player begins an inning and shoots until missing, committing a foul, or wining. The game ends when the 9-ball is pocketed on a legal shot, or the game is forfeited for a serious infraction of the rules.

5.5. PUSH OUT. The player who shoots the shot immediately after a legal break may play a push out in an attempt to move the cue ball into a better position for the option that follows. On a push out, the cue ball is not required to contact any object ball nor any rail, but all other foul rules still apply. The player must announce the intention of playing a push out before the shot, or the shot is considered to be a normal shot. Any ball pocketed on the push out does not count and remains pocketed except the 9-ball. Following a legal push out, the incoming player is permitted to shoot from that position or to pass the shot back to the player who pushed out. A push out is not considered to be a foul as long as no rule (*except rules 5.7 and 5.8*) is violated. An illegal push out is penalized according to the type of foul committed. After a player scratches on the break shot, the incoming player cannot play a push out.

5.6. FOULS. When a player commits a foul, he must relinquish his run at the table and no balls pocketed on the foul shot are respotted (*exception: if a pocketed ball is the 9-ball, it is respotted*). The incoming player is awarded ball in hand; prior to his first shot he may place the cue ball anywhere on the table. If a player commits several fouls on one shot, they are counted as only one foul.

5.7. BAD HIT. If the first object ball contacted by the cue ball is not the lowest-numbered ball on the table, the shot is a foul.

6

5.8. NO RAIL. If no object ball is pocketed, failure to drive the cue ball or any numbered ball to a rail after the cue ball contacts the object ball, is a foul.

5.9. IN HAND. When the cue ball is in hand, the player may place the cue ball anywhere on the bed of the table, except in contact with an object ball. The player may continue to adjust the position of the cue ball until shooting.

5.10. OBJECT BALLS JUMPED OFF THE TABLE. An unpocketed ball is considered to be driven off the table if it comes to rest other than on the bed of the table. It is a foul to drive an object ball off the table. The jumped object ball(s) is not respotted (*exception: if the object ball is the 9-ball, it is respotted*) and play continues.

5.11. JUMP AND MASSE SHOT FOUL. If a match is not refereed, it will be considered a cue ball foul if during an attempt to jump, curve or massé the cue ball over or around an impeding numbered ball, the impeding ball moves (*regardless of whether it was moved by hand, cue stick follow-through or bridge*).

5.12. THREE CONSECUTIVE FOULS. If a player fouls three consecutive times on three successive shots without making an intervening legal shot, the game is lost. The three fouls must occur in one game. The warning must be given between the second and third fouls. A player's inning begins when it is legal to take a shot and ends at the end of a shot in which he misses, fouls or wins, or when he fouls between shots.

5.13. END OF GAME. A game starts as soon as the cue ball crosses over the head string on the opening break. The 1-ball must be legally contacted on the break shot. The game ends at the end of a legal shot which pockets the 9-ball, or when a player forfeits the game as a result of a foul.

♦ ♦ ♦

CHAPTER 2

BREAK SHOT

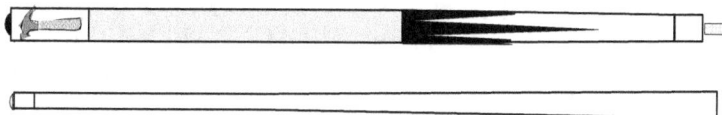

A ll pool games start with some sort of break shot. Depending on the type of game being played, the break shot is either a defensive (ONE-POCKET) or an offensive shot. The break shot in NINE-BALL is usually an offensive shot, that is, an attempt is made at making a ball so the shooter can continue to shoot. The importance of the break shot in NINE-BALL increases with the skill level of the players.

Of all shots in NINE-BALL, the break shot will benefit most from a thorough, logical analysis. The break shot is easy to analyze because unlike most other shots, all the balls are in a prescribed position before the shot is executed.

Keep in mind; there is no reason you can't break as well as a professional pool player. You don't need great strategy skills, and you don't have to plan three balls in advance. You can do as well as the pros by absorbing everything in this chapter, then practice until it becomes automatic.

9

♦ ♦ ♦

LAG FOR BREAK

Before you get to break the balls you must win that privilege. When playing EIGHT-BALL a flip of a coin is generally used to determine who breaks the balls. In the game of NINE-BALL a lag shot is generally used to determine who breaks in the first game of a match.

As used here, the term *"lag shot"* refers to a specific shot in which a ball is shot from behind the head string to the foot rail and back to the head rail. Both players shoot the lag shot at the same time. The person whose ball stops closest to the head rail wins the lag shot.

In any specific match, the fewer number of wins required to win the match, the more important the lag shot is. In matches where the rules dictate that the winner breaks each succeeding game, winning the lag shot is worth more than if the break shot is alternated. The better the players are, the more important the break shot is, and consequently so is the lag shot.

The lag shot is the first shot to be executed in a match. The players may not have executed a shot for a while so they may be a little jittery. The players are anticipating the combat, so anxiety is at its highest level. Action hasn't started yet so the mental focus hasn't fully developed. For these reasons, players will generally be at their worst when executing the lag shot. When practicing the lag shot, it is not unusual for a person to be able to consistently stop the ball within three or four inches of the head rail. The same person may have trouble stopping the ball within one diamond (12 inches) of the rail in an actual match. Some practice lag shots should be included in any pre-game warm up routine.

Because of poor cushion efficiency (typically about 40%), you should try to shoot hard enough so the ball rebounds off the foot rail and **strikes** the cushion on the head rail about 70 percent of the time. In other words: to minimize your average error, you should come up short of the head rail no more than 30 percent of the time. For a complete analysis of this concept see Chapter 11 in the book *THE SCIENCE OF POCKET BILLIARDS.*

The lag shot is the only shot in pool where both players shoot at the same time. This can be extremely unnerving. The problem is you know you should shoot at about the same time as your opponent. Since you don't know when your opponent is going to shoot you don't know when you are going to shoot. It's a little disconcerting to have your opponent in control of your timing. You don't want to deliberately shoot first because this might cause you to rush your shot. Yet, you don't want to shoot second and be forced to rush your shot just to catch up. So what's a shooter to do?

The best way to maintain control and avoid indecision on the lag shot is to shoot **on a count**. Once you settle into your shooting stance, start counting your preliminary strokes. Shoot after a specific number of strokes; three, five or whatever you decide is most comfortable for you. When you

11

use the counting system you should establish a personalized mental routine. For example, with each preliminary stroke say to yourself:

"One—to that cushion and stop 3 inches past this cushion."
"Two—speed is my only concern."
"Three—hear and feel the shot."
"Four—back to this cushion you go" -- as you execute the shot.

Once you decide on your personal routine, use it consistently both in practice and in competition. This technique will keep **you** in complete control. Shooting alongside your opponent will no longer have a detrimental influence on the timing and speed of your lag shot.

Since two players are shooting at the same time, two balls must be used for the lag shot. Occasionally the cue ball and one of the object balls are used for this purpose. This creates a problem because the surface of the cue ball and object ball are different. The cue ball is continually being struck with the chalked cue tip caucusing microscopic pits and scratches on its surface. These pits and scratches cause high friction between the ball and cushion. When the cue ball strikes the foot cushion the high friction causes the ball's rotation to stop and it is subsequently rebounded back with little or no rotation. The friction between the smooth object ball and cushion is less; therefore, its forward rotation is not completely stopped as it rebounds from the foot rail. Consequently, it rebounds back while still rotating forward. Rotating in the opposite direction of its movement causes it to decelerate rapidly. The rapid deceleration causes it to rebound a shorter distance than the cue ball (presuming they both had the same initial speed). Therefore, the person that lags with the cue ball has an advantage because he/she is more familiar with the response of the cue ball off a cushion. To be fair, both players should use object balls (or preferably cue balls) for the lag shot.

> Note: Winning the lag, and getting the break shot, gives the first shooter a psychological advantage. Your opponent is disappointed even before the game starts and at the same time you're elated. Also, the first shot of the match is the most tense part of the game. If you get to swing with wild abandon (power break shot) it is much more settling than having to finesse your very first shot.

◆◆◆

BREAK OBJECTIVES

We can <u>hope for</u> some things to happen on the break shot and <u>play for</u> others.

Hope for:
1. <u>Make the 9-ball</u>: Of course, in the best of all worlds the 9-ball would go in on the break. Under most rules this would be a win and no other objectives would be needed. However, since the 9-

ball doesn't go in very often, we must have alternative objectives.

2. <u>Make any ball</u>: We can hope that at least one, and hopefully more, random balls will go into a pocket.

3. <u>Scatter</u>: Along with making a ball we hope all the balls are scattered so running them will not require breaking up clusters.

Play for:

1. <u>Make a wing ball</u>: The two balls that are closest to the side rails (when racked) are usually referred to as "wing balls" or "corner balls." One of these wing balls can often be deliberately made into a corner pocket on the foot rail.

2. <u>Make the 1-ball</u>: When breaking from the side of the table, the 1-ball can be played for the opposite side pocket.

3. <u>Get shape</u>: Usually, you want the cue ball to end up in the middle of the table. This position gives you the highest odds of getting a shot at the next ball.

Depending on how the balls are breaking, you may want to fine-tune your objectives. If the wing ball is going in consistently, and the 1-ball ends up near the head rail, you may want to draw the cue ball back toward the head rail for better shape on the 1-ball.

If the 1-ball is consistently made in the side pocket, you should try to position the cue ball for a good shot at the 2-ball. The desired cue ball position will vary depending on where the 2-ball is positioned in the rack. Where the 2-ball (or any other ball) will most likely end up will be discussed later in this chapter.

♦ ♦ ♦

RACKING THE BALLS

For a consistent break, it is important that all the balls are in contact with the adjacent balls, they are racked in the proper position on the table, and the rack is aligned properly.

The standard triangular 15 ball rack is generally used for racking the nine balls. Diamond shaped racks (with space for only nine balls) are available but are rarely used. The problems with using a diamond shaped rack are: the difficulty of pushing the balls forward (can't get fingers behind the rear balls) and the rack is difficult to remove without disturbing the balls.

According to the rules, there are only two balls that have a predetermined position in the rack. The 1-ball must be in the front of the pack and the 9-ball must be in the center. The person doing the racking has the option of putting the other balls in any position.

The mechanics of racking -- When racking, all nine balls are pushed forward in the rack with the thumbs and knuckles. While the balls are held in position, the rack and balls are moved into the proper position on the table. When the center of the 1-ball is positioned directly on the foot spot, the balls are

15

released and the rack removed. To remove the rack, slide it forward slightly then lift the back end while arching it forward. All the balls must remain in place and in contact with each adjacent ball after the rack has been removed.

Racking problems -- It is almost impossible to get a perfect rack of balls. Even after the balls have been pushed forward in the rack, small gaps between balls may exist. As an experiment, try this: Push all the balls forward in the rack; now release the balls but hold the rack in place. To test how tight they are, use the tip of your finger to gently push forward on the rearmost ball. Any perceptible movement of the balls indicates an imperfection in the rack. If you detect imperfections, move the rack and balls toward the foot cushion then back again; test them again for tightness.

Obviously it is quite difficult to rack the balls tight even when they are still in the rack. Compounding the problem, when the rack is removed the balls quite frequently move creating gaps between balls. Even if the balls don't move, there may be gaps caused by balls that aren't spherical or balls that are different sizes.

Note: There are no perfect racks because the balls themselves are not perfect. So, a good rack is a matter of degree. And that is how it should be—consider how boring the break would be if the balls always ended up in the same position.

Over time a low spot may develop in the cloth at the foot spot (this is more likely to occur if a "spot patch" is not used). The low spot may even develop into a hole after a long period of time. Because of the low spot, the 1-ball sometimes won't stay in place when the rack is removed. If the 1-ball settles into the hole it will be lower than the cue ball when they make contact. This will cause the cue ball to bounce up on impact and not transfer all of its energy to the pack. When a low spot develops on the foot spot it may be necessary to rack the balls slightly forward of the foot spot. However, both players should agree as to where the 1-ball will be positioned.

A line, drawn from the center of the 1-ball to the center of the ball at the rear of the pack, must be parallel to the side cushions. This alignment is generally left up to the racker's judgment. However, it is much easier to align the rack accurately if there is a line drawn, on the table, from the center of the foot spot back toward the foot rail. The line can be observed between the balls, from above, while racking. When the rack is adjusted so the line is directly down the center of the rack, the balls will be aligned perfectly.

Irregularities in the cloth may occasionally cause one or more perimeter balls to move when the rack is removed. Rubbing the cloth, in the offending area, with the hand or towel can often rectify this problem. If wiping the cloth doesn't work try pushing the offending ball down into the nape and rotating it in the direction of the 9-ball. If nothing else works, the offending ball(s) should be held in place and tapped lightly with another ball. Be careful not to tap too hard because the threads in the cloth are likely to be cut eventually resulting in a hole. When a ball is tapped into position it will be slightly lower than the adjacent balls; therefore, the pack will not react predictably (there may be some bouncing and jumping within the pack) when the cue ball slams into the 1-ball.

Variation in ball size and sphericity can cause gaps even when the balls are being pushed forward in the rack. If variation in ball size is the problem, exchanging ball positions sometimes helps. If the gaps are caused by sphericity imperfections, try rotating the balls. If moving balls and/or rotating balls does not eliminate the gaps, pick the best side to break from and try to use the gaps to your advantage.

Note: Occasionally, a set of balls may have one or more balls that are slightly off-size. These off-sized balls will cause gaps that are nearly impossible to correct. If the 1-ball is 10 thousandths of an inch oversize, it will cause a gap 14 thousandths of an inch between the second two balls. If an off-size ball is placed in the rear most position, its size won't matter much. If an off-size ball is positioned anywhere else in the pack it will cause gaps between balls.

If the 9-ball is off-size, one of the other striped balls (10 through 15) should be used as a substitute.

◆ ◆ ◆

RACK ANALYSIS

Most people think it is the *table* that determines the type of action you get on the break shot. Actually the *balls* are much more of a determining factor. How tightly the balls are racked and the friction between adjacent balls are the most important factors.

Gaps between balls cause an irregular *shock wave propagation*. (For a comprehensive examination of shock wave propagation, and the effects of gaps between balls, the reader is referred to the book *UPSCALE ONE-POCKET*.) In short, when gaps are present the balls have a greater tendency to run back into each other after they initially begin moving. When this happens some energy is lost and consequently the balls don't move as far.

Friction between balls determines the amount of *collision-induced throw* and the amount of throw determines (to some extent) what direction a ball will go after being struck by another ball. Therefore, changing the ball-to-ball friction will change the way the balls react on the break shot. Friction variances may be caused by how dirty or polished the balls are or even humidity conditions. Some players may have oil or powder on their hands which could be transferred to the balls while racking. These friction variables may change from day to day, game to game, or even during a game. As those variables change, the reaction of the balls to the break shot will change.

In some cases an imperfection in the rack may be to the breakers advantage. Occasionally there may be one ball that just won't stay in place; try breaking from different cue-ball positions, there may be a

19

place on the table that will allow you to make balls that you wouldn't normally make with a tight rack. When the balls are racked perfectly tight the 9-ball is very difficult to make. Any rack imperfection makes it easier to make (or at least move) the 9-ball. If the rack is angled to one side it may help to pocket the 1-ball or a wing ball. The same is true if the 1-ball is positioned ahead or behind the foot spot. Remember, don't complain—exploit.

♦ ♦ ♦

AIMING POINT

Ideally, on the break shot, the cue ball should transfer all of its energy to the pack. In order for this to happen the cue ball must strike the 1-ball head-on. The more the cue ball deviates from a head-on collision the less energy is transferred to the pack.

Striking the 1-ball head-on is best in nearly all situations. However in some cases a slight off-center hit may help pocket the 1-ball or wing ball.

When adjusting aim to either side of the 1-ball, it is best to pick out a specific point in the pack that represents the aiming point. This aim point can be the center or edge of any ball behind the 1-ball. Having a specific aim point allows for consistency.

For most shots the visual focus should be on the object ball during the final stroke. The break shot is an exception to this rule. The initial focus should be on the aim point, then, at the last second, focus should switch to the cue ball.

♦♦♦

ENGLISH

Top english -- Some players advise using top english on the break shot so the cue ball drives forward after striking the pack. Supposedly, the cue ball has a second chance at driving another ball into a pocket. There are several flaws in this reasoning. Putting top english on the cue ball means some of the energy contained in the stick was used to rotate the cue ball. This means less energy was delegated to linear movement (less velocity). With top english the cue ball strikes the pack then stops; most of the rotational energy is lost to friction as it spins on the cloth while trying to accelerate forward. And, there are more problems; after stopping, the cue ball never really gains enough speed to be of much help in knocking another ball into a pocket. It actually enters a zone where there are several object balls moving at a high velocity. It is quite likely that the cue ball will get in the way of a fast moving object ball, thereby reducing its speed and likelihood of going into a pocket. Also, the cue ball gets ricocheted about which increases its chance of going into a pocket.

Bottom english -- Some players advise using bottom english so the cue ball backs up to the middle of the table. In order for the cue ball to be struck below center, it is necessary to elevate the butt of the stick. A slightly elevated stick is of little concern for most shots but the situation is a little different for the break shot. The cue ball is struck so hard that it bounces off the table bed. If the cue ball is above the bed of the table when it strikes the 1-ball it will ricochet even higher (it may even fly off the table). And there is another problem; if the cue ball is not on the table when it strikes the 1-ball it will not transfer all of its energy to the pack.

♦ ♦ ♦

CUE-BALL PLACEMENT

The rules dictate that the cue ball can be positioned anywhere behind the head string for the break shot. The player usually selects a cue-ball placement based on; how well the balls are breaking from various positions, handedness, rack imperfections, and/or preferred bridge type. Some players break from the same place on the table regardless how the balls are breaking. Other players move the cue ball around to experimentally find the placement that produces the best results.

Note: In the succeeding discussion, pertaining to the racked balls, the individual balls will be assumed to be initially racked in the positions shown in **Figure 2-1**. The cue ball placement will be anywhere from the *center* to the extreme *right* side of the table.

Cue ball near side rail -- Most players break from the side of the table and use a rail bridge. Generally, the closer to the side the cue ball is placed, the greater the chance of making the 1-ball in the side pocket and the right side wing ball (4-ball in **Figure 2-1**) in the right corner pocket. The exact placement, relative to the rail, depends largely on the mechanics of the stroke. The closer to the cushion the cue ball is placed the more the butt of the cue stick must be elevated in order to strike the cue ball in the center. The higher the butt end is raised the more the cue ball will bounce. (The problem with bouncing the cue ball will be discussed later in this chapter.) And, the closer the cue ball is to the rail, the shorter the bridge distance must be (providing the cue shaft is resting on the rail). The shorter the bridge distance, the less power that can be produced. When the cue ball is adjacent to the cushion the bridge distance will only be about 5 inches. As the cue ball is moved away from the cushion the bridge distance increased. When the cue ball is 6 inches from the side cushion the bridge distance will be about 18 inches.

The shorter the bridge distance the easier it is to hit the cue ball where desired. The longer the bridge distance the more power that can be generated. The breaker must decide on a compromise between hitting the cue ball accurately and generating maximum power. Most professionals position the center of the cue ball just behind the head string about 4 inches from the side cushion. This position requires a bridge distance of about 14 inches.

Figure 2-1 shows the direction each ball goes when the 1-ball is struck head-on from a cue ball placement just behind the head string and 4 inches from the side cushion.

1-BALL -- Breaking from the side allows the 1-ball to escape to the side after being pinned between the cue ball and 3-ball. This allows it to go toward the side pocket. When the 1-ball is struck head-on it will strike the cushion just short of the side pocket. If the 1-ball misses the side pocket it usually ends up near the head rail. The 1-ball is the second most frequently made ball.

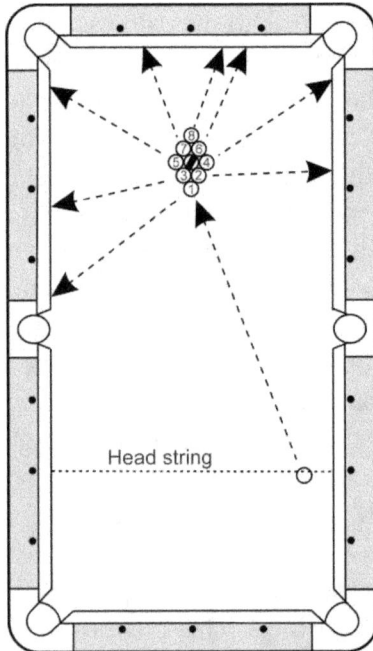

Figure 2-1. Ball exit direction when breaking from the side.

2-BALL -- The 2-ball moves the least of all the balls except for the 9-ball. It usually moves almost directly toward the right side cushion and, if it isn't struck by another ball it stays near that cushion. The 2-ball is sometimes struck by the 8-ball as it rebounds off the end rail.

3-BALL -- The 3-ball strikes the side rail a few inches past the second diamond from the foot of the table. It doesn't travel very fast and is rarely made. It generally isn't involved in any secondary collisions. The direction of the 3-ball doesn't change much even when the 1-ball is struck to either side of center.

4-BALL -- The 4-ball is the most frequently made ball and is the second fastest ball out of the rack. It sometimes goes into the right corner pocket but usually strikes the side cushion an inch or so from the pocket. Even if it doesn't go directly into the corner pocket, it may go in after colliding with the 5-, 6-, or 8-ball.

5-BALL -- The 5-ball is all important because it *stirs the pot*. The 5-ball is the fastest ball out of the pack and therefore moves a great distance and is involved in many collisions. It usually strikes the side cushion about 3 or 4 inches from the left corner pocket. It rebounds from the side cushion and may run into the 4-, 6-, or 8-ball. It may carom off one of these balls and go into the right corner pocket or knock one of the other balls into that pocket.

Note: Since there are so many collisions near the right corner pocket it receives more balls, on the break, than any of the other pockets.

6-BALL -- The 6-ball comes out of the pack in the same general direction as the 8-ball but at a slower speed. The 8-ball sometimes comes off the foot rail and runs into the 6-ball. The 6-ball may also be struck by the 4- or 5-ball as they come off cushions. The 6-ball goes in the same general direction regardless of how the 1-ball is struck.

7-BALL -- The 7-ball doesn't do much. It comes out of the pack slowly and isn't involved in many secondary collisions. On rare occasions it may help carom the 9-ball into the left corner pocket.

8-BALL -- The 8-ball is the third most makeable ball (after the 4- and 1-ball). It strikes the foot cushion and goes toward the right corner pocket at the head of the table. If the 1-ball is struck off-center, the 8-ball has a greater tendency to get involved in secondary collisions near the foot cushion.

9-BALL -- The 9-ball moves out of the pack at the slowest speed of all the balls. It frequently doesn't even move but when it does it is usually a feeble move toward the left corner pocket.

Cue ball placement in the center of the table --
When breaking from the center of the table (striking the 1-ball head-on) the balls should break symmetrically. That is, the balls that leave the pack on the left side should go in the same direction as the balls on the right side of the pack. The fact that this

doesn't happen very often in real life is an indication of the effects of gaps between balls, the variation in friction between balls, and ball irregularities.

Figure 2-2 shows the direction each ball goes when the 1-ball is struck head-on from the center of the table. Note that none of the balls break toward a pocket. When a ball is pocketed from this cue ball position it is the result of a collision with another ball and/or rebound off a cushion.

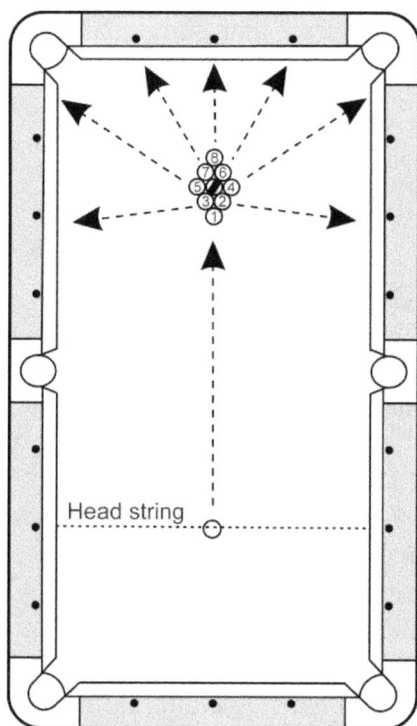

FIGURE 2-2. Ball exit direction when breaking from the center of the table.

The 1-ball and the 9-ball don't move much when the shot is executed perfectly. However, the 8-ball will generally rebound off the end cushion and strike the 9- and 1-ball. Also, if the 1-ball is misstruck the 2- or 3-ball could rebound off a cushion and carom into the 1- and/or 9-ball. The 4- and 5-ball both come off the side cushions at a high rate of speed and may carom into the 6-, 7-, or 8-ball.

Breaking from anywhere between the center and side rail will cause the balls to go in a direction somewhere between that shown in **Figure 2-1** and **Figure 2-2**.

◆ ◆ ◆

STRIKING 1-BALL
OFF-CENTER

As mentioned earlier, the 1-ball must be struck head-on in order to transfer all of the cue ball's energy to the pack. If all of the cue ball's energy is not passed to the pack the cue ball will rebound around the table after impact with the 1-ball. This is not only wasted energy but also increases its chance of going into a pocket (a foul). A foul on the break gives the opponent ball-in-hand which is a considerable advantage. With all this in mind, there are still some instances where striking the 1-ball off-center may still be a viable alternative technique.

It should be noted that when breaking from the center of the table, the 1-ball can be struck off-center enough so that the contact point on the 1-ball is the same as it would be if it were shot head-on from the side of the table. In this case the balls in the rack will act as though the 1-ball was struck head-on from the side. That is, the 1-ball will go toward the side pocket and the 4-ball will go toward the corner pocket. The problem is that only a portion of the cue ball's energy will be transferred to the pack. Reducing the pack's energy is detrimental because the object balls do not move as far.

Note: Professional players are so good at making the wing ball that at one point a professional organization disallowed breaking from within 16 inches of the side rail.

On some occasions, when breaking from the side, the 1-ball consistently strikes the left side cushion an inch or so short of the side pocket. Striking the 1-ball 0.025 inch (half the thickness of a dime) off-center will change its striking point about an inch at the side pocket. This type of minor aim adjustment is justified because it diminishes the energy transfer only slightly while significantly increasing the chance of making the 1-ball.

The same kind of aim adjustment can be made to help make the wing ball into the right corner pocket. If the wing ball consistently strikes the side rail an inch or so from the corner pocket, striking the 1-ball to the right of center will increase its chance of going in. However, the amount of correction is much more than that needed to change the direction of the 1-ball. It may be necessary to strike the 1-ball as much as a half inch to the right to affect the wing ball's direction one inch at the pocket. This may not be desirable because the cue ball will run wild after striking the 1-ball.

Or, you can throw all the rules to the wind and break in a drastically different way: When breaking from the right side, aim for a three quarter ball hit on the left side of the 1-ball (try to shoot the 1-ball into the center of the foot rail). With just a trace of bottom the cue ball will go to the side cushion and come back through the center of the pack. With this break, the 9-ball usually moves on initial impact. But, if it doesn't, the cue ball may strike it as it comes back through the pack area. The rear most ball (8-ball) may also strike the end cushion and rebound back through the pack area. Care must be taken not to make the cue ball jump because it could easily fly off the table. This break may be best suited to those players that, for some physical reason, can't hit the cue ball very hard.

♦♦♦

IMPERFECT RACK

It is nearly impossible to get a perfect rack of balls every time. The rack may be aligned improperly, the 1-ball may not be perfectly on the foot spot, or there may be tiny gaps between balls. Some of the imperfections help and some hinder the breaker.

In the following analyses only the initial movement of the balls are considered. There may be some advantages or disadvantages that occur after the balls contact other balls or multiple rails.

Rack alignment -- An improper rack alignment is nearly always to the benefit of the breaker. In the following analysis the rear most ball (8-ball) is presumed to be positioned to the **left** of where it should be. Of course, the mirror image action of this rack would also apply to this analysis.

When the rack is askew to the left it is generally easier to make the 4-ball in the right corner pocket by breaking from the right rail. This is because the 4-ball usually strikes the side cushion an inch or so from the pocket. With the rack skewed to the left the 4-ball will strike the side cushion closer to (or perhaps in) the pocket. Obviously, if the rack were skewed to the right it would be best to break from the left side in order to make to wing ball (in this case the 5-ball).

When breaking from the side, if the 1-ball normally strikes the cushion an inch or so short of the side pocket, the skewed rack (to the left) will cause it to strike closer (or into) the side pocket.

In some cases, depending on the surface characteristics of the balls, the rearmost ball (8-ball) may be easier to bank into the right corner pocket on the head rail. However, the cue-ball position may have to be adjusted to take advantage of this imperfection.

Off foot spot -- There usually develops an indent or hole in the cloth on the foot spot where the 1-ball is positioned. This is because the 1-ball is usually being struck above center, which drives it down into the cloth (more on this later). This downward force is similar to poundings on the 1-ball with a hammer;

eventually the cloth will develop an indent or hole at that point.

If the balls are racked such that the 1-ball is sitting in an indentation; the cue ball may bounce up into the air on impact with the pack. This will result in a very inefficient break even when the shooter has done everything properly. For this reason it may be necessary to rack the balls a little in front of or behind the indentation.

If the 1-ball is in front of the foot spot (toward the head of the table) the 1-ball will generally have a better chance of going into the side pocket but the 4-ball (wing ball) will be more difficult to make. However, if the 1-ball is positioned behind the foot spot, the wing ball will be slightly easier to make.

Gaps between balls -- Because of the many variables it is difficult to study the effects of gaps between balls on the break shot. Gaps caused by a variation in ball size will cause a different reaction than gaps caused by a ball being out of position. And, when there is one gap there is almost certainly one or more secondary gaps. Primary gaps, secondary gaps, and breaking position all combine in affecting the way the balls break. The following analyses are general and should be used only as a guide in assessing a rack of balls that have gaps.

Note: In the following analyses it is assumed that the balls are racked in the order shown in **Figure 6-1**. It is also assumed that the 1-ball is struck head-on from the right side of the table.

Primary gaps between:

1-ball and 2-ball: The 5- and 8-ball come out normally. That is about the only thing that is normal about this break. The 6-ball goes farther to the right than normal. The rest of the balls move much less than normal. This is what is usually called a *mud rack*. The reason that this gap affects the rack so much is that normally most of the ball action is on the right side. With the gap being on the right side everything gets screwed up.

1-ball and 3-ball: The 1-ball comes out much faster than normal and strikes the side cushion farther toward the foot of the table than normal. The 3-ball comes out slower than usual.

2-ball and 3-ball: The 2-ball comes out slower and slightly farther up-table.

2-ball and 4-ball: The 2-ball moves a little faster than normal. The 4-ball strikes the side cushion farther from the corner pocket.

3-ball and 5-ball: The 3-ball strikes the side cushion several inches farther toward the side pocket than normal. The 1-ball strikes the side rail farther toward the head of the table.

4-ball and 6-ball: The 4-ball goes farther toward the end rail. The 9-ball moves toward the left corner pocket.

5-ball and 7-ball: The 5- and 7-ball are not affected much. The 6- and 8-ball go more toward the right.

6-ball and 8-ball: The 8-ball comes out much faster and farther to the right than normal. The 6-ball comes out slower and strikes farther to the left than normal. The rest of the balls act as they do normally.

7-ball and 8-ball: The 8-ball comes out a little faster than normal and gets away from the collisions with the 4-, 5-, and 6- ball.

Gaps around the 9-ball are usually secondary gaps caused by gaps around the perimeter, which have already have been discussed.

◆ ◆ ◆

CUE-BALL ACTION

Cue-ball bounce -- Most people try to strike the cue ball near the center on the break shot. In order to strike the cue ball in the center, the cue stick must be held such that the butt end is slightly above the tip end. Shooting down at the cue ball causes it to jump as it is propelled away.

The harder the cue ball is struck the higher and farther it will bounce. When the cue ball comes back down to the table it doesn't stay there, it continues to bounce until the vertical component of its energy is exhausted. Because the cue ball continues to bounce, there is a good chance that it may be in the air when it strikes the 1-ball. If it is in the air when it contacts the 1-ball it will carom even higher into the air.

If the break shot is repeated over and over from the same starting position the cue ball will start to leave a light colored mark, on the cloth, where it comes down after the first bounce. The cue ball landing marks can be easily seen on tables at professional pool tournaments with new cloth. At men's tournaments the track starts about 1/2 diamond past the center string, at women's tournaments it starts nearer the center string. The difference is probably the result of how hard the cue ball is hit.

There are several reasons why it is undesirable to strike the 1-ball when the cue ball is in the air: (1) All the energy contained in the cue ball will not be transferred to the pack because it imparts a glancing blow. If the cue ball bounces one foot in the air after striking the 1-ball it is like losing about 75 feet of rolling distance (neglecting cushion efficiency). (2) The cue ball may glance off the 1-ball and fly off the table, or, it may cause an object ball to fly off the table. And (3) the cue ball and 1-ball will both have a smaller effective diameter at the collision point. Therefore, any error in aim will be magnified.

Figure 2-3 shows several bouncing patterns the cue ball may assume. In 2-**3A** the cue ball is coming down into the 1-ball. The cue ball loses energy trying to pound the 1-ball into the table. This not only results in a poor break but it causes an indentation in the cloth below the 1-ball. In 2-**3B** the cue ball bounces but is on the table when it strikes the 1-ball. This results in a strong break and all the balls stay on the table. In 2-**3C** the cue ball takes two bounces before reaching the pack but is on the table when it

35

contacts the pack. Even with the extra bounce there is an efficient transfer of energy from the cue ball to the pack. In 2-**3D** the cue ball lands on the table just before striking the pack and is in the process of bouncing into the air as it strikes the pack. This is the worst of all scenarios because not only is a lot of energy wasted but the cue ball will probably fly off the table.

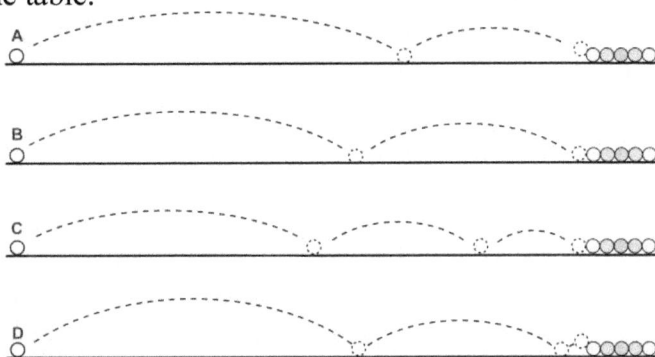

FIGURE 2-3. The cue ball bounces on its way to the pack.

Obviously, a bouncing cue ball is usually not a good thing. So what can be done to avoid the problems caused by a bouncing cue ball? Most experts advise slowing down the power-break stroke. This generally works but it has its downside. While the efficiency of the transfer of energy from the cue ball to the pack may improve, there is less energy to begin with. There are several other things that can be tried before resorting to slowing down the stroke.

Bridge type -- (In this analysis the bridge distance is assumed to be 15 inches and the cue ball is struck in the center.) When using a side rail bridge, with the shaft resting on the rail, the closer the cue ball is to the cushion the more the cue stick must be inclined downward and consequently the higher the cue ball will bounce. If the cue ball is 4 inches from the side cushion, the cue stick must be inclined downward nearly 5 degrees in order to strike the cue ball in the center. If the cue ball is progressively moved closer to the rail, the stick-incline increases significantly.

If the cue-ball placement is just behind the head string and is far enough from the rail so that a table bridge is used, the stick incline will be less than with the rail bridge. The exact incline will depend on how high above the rail the stick is when contact with the cue ball is made. The stick incline will be 2.4 degrees (about half that of a rail bridge) if the stick is held such that it clears the rail by 1/4 inch. If it is held such that it clears the rail by 1/2 inch (about average for this type of bridge) the stick incline will be 3.0 degrees.

If an end rail bridge is used (with the cue shaft resting on the rail 15 inches away from the cue ball) the stick incline will be 2.6 degrees.

It is apparent that in changing the bridge type the bounce characteristics will change because of changing stick incline.

Bridge distance -- A slight change in bridge distance will change the incline of the stick and in turn change the bounce characteristics of the cue ball. For example changing the end rail bridge from 15 inches to 10 inches would change the stick incline from 2.6 degrees to 3.7 degrees. Changing the stick incline even one degree doesn't sound like much but it will significantly change the bounce characteristics and consequent break efficiency.

Distance to the pack -- Occasionally you need only change the distance between the cue ball and the pack to insure that the cue ball is on the table when it impacts the 1-ball. For example, assume the player is breaking from immediately behind the head string one diamond out from the rail. Assume the cue ball is bouncing such that it would come down to the table surface three inches behind the 1-ball. If the player moved the cue ball to a position three inches behind the head string, the cue ball will be on the table when it strikes the 1-ball.

Change sides -- Frequently, just changing the cue ball position from one side of the table to the other will change the bounce characteristics. This is because subtle differences in where the table and rails are, in relation to the body, will induce a slightly different stroke or striking point on the cue ball.

Note: Keep in mind that for any specific cue-ball placement, the cue-ball distance to the 1-ball will vary depending on the size of the table. If a person were to land the cue ball just at impact on a large table, the same relative cue ball placement would produce different results on a small table.

Strike point on cue ball -- Some experts advise striking the cue ball slightly below center so that it backs up to the center of the table after striking the 1-ball. This advice is based on the theory that the cue ball stops after it runs into the 1-ball and requires top or bottom english in order to accelerate either forward or backwards. The hypothesis for this theory is not totally accurate. In the real world, the cue ball gets rebounded back off the 1-ball after impact. This is because the 1-ball strikes two balls (2- and 3-ball) <u>at the same time</u>, which keeps it from moving as much as expected. Because the 1-ball doesn't move much it recoils back into the cue ball. As a result of being struck by the 1-ball the cue ball is propelled back up-table. This means that bottom english is not required to get the cue ball to move toward the head of the table. If bottom english is not used, then the stick can be held closer to level, which translates to less cue ball bounce.

There are times when it is not desirable for the cue ball to end up in the center of the table. For example, if the 1-ball consistently goes into the side pocket you may want to go for shape on the 2-ball. You can sometimes judge where the 2-ball will end up by where it is in the pack. Or, if the wing ball consistently goes into the corner pocket and the 1-ball ends up near the head rail, you will want the cue ball to end up near the head rail also.

Slow down -- As a last resort, you may have to slow the speed of your power break to avoid bounce problems. On the surface, this does not seem like very good advice, but it may have some legitimacy—especially if you are able to gain accuracy and consistency by slowing down.

39

In some circumstances, by increasing aim accuracy, the 1-ball can be made more frequently. If you can consistently make the 1-ball at a certain speed then don't try to make additional balls by shooting harder. Just try to get shape on the 2-ball wherever you expect it to be.

Bounce test -- In order to correct a bounce problem it usually helps if you can actually see where the cue ball is hitting the table. To experiment with your individual break: Tape three or four sheets of 8½ by 11 white paper together end to end. Tape an equal number of sheets of carbon paper together in the same way. Lightly tape the white paper to the table starting at the 1-ball and going toward the cue ball starting position. Lay the carbon paper over the white paper and you are ready to experiment. When executing the power-break shot, the cue ball will leave a mark on the white paper each time it lands on the table. The farther apart the marks are the higher the jump and/or the faster the cue ball is traveling.

Be careful in your analysis of the marks; most people erroneously think that the farther the first mark is from the starting position the better. While a long distance to the first mark may be an indication of fast speed (which is good), it may also indicate a high bounce (which is bad). Some indication of the relative height of the bounce can be determined by the darkness of the mark. The more pronounced (darker) the mark, the higher the bounce.

The most important information the marks provide is an indication of whether or not the cue ball is on the table when it strikes the 1-ball.

Note: In shooting the break shot, for the bounce test, it is not necessary to shoot at a full rack of balls. Shooting at a single ball on the spot is not good either because it will bounce off the table if struck by a cue ball that is not on the table at impact. The solution is to place a ball on the foot spot and another ball right behind it.

◆ ◆ ◆

STANCE AND STROKE

With the normal shooting stance, the chin should be fairly close to the stick. This allows for maximum aim accuracy and adequate power for most shots. The emphasis with the power-break shot is on **speed**; therefore, the body should be more upright allowing greater freedom of arm movement and extreme follow-through. The initial aiming process can start with the chin near the stick, but before the final power stroke, the body should be moved into a more upright position. The stick should be griped tighter than normal and held several inches nearer the butt end.

Note: Be sure to wear shoes that don't slip on the floor. Can you imagine breaking while wearing roller skates?

The cue stick should accelerate throughout the break stroke. Because terminal speed is a function of acceleration, bridge distance affects stick speed exponentially. In other words, a slight increase in bridge distance increases the stick speed (at impact with the cue ball) tremendously. **Therefore, the bridge distance should be as <u>long</u> as possible to allow time for the stick to accelerate before striking the cue ball.** Think small—even a half inch increase in bridge distance will increase power considerably.

> Consider this: Most pool players break at less than 20 miles per hour. Softball pitchers are able to pitch a ball at over 100 miles per hour. The motion they use is similar to the pool player except they have a longer wind-up (stroke).

The limiting factor for bridge distance is being able to strike the cue ball where desired. The longer the bridge distance, the less accurately the cue ball can be struck. In practicing the break shot, the bridge distance should be increased in small increments until the cue ball is misstruck about 10 percent of the time. In actual play, shorten this maximum bridge distance slightly to insure an accurate hit on the cue ball. Most players miscue less frequently when they have their <u>visual focus on the cue ball</u> during the stroke rather than on the aim point. Having the visual focus on the cue ball will allow a longer bridge distance without miscuing.

A common mistake made by novices and professionals alike is not using the entire bridge distance. Starting the final power stroke with the cue tip several inches in front of the bridge is counterproductive. Aim accuracy is lost because of the long bridge while gaining no benefit in added speed.

To maximize the advantage of a long bridge you should be able to **see the ferrule on the back side of the bridge on the final back stroke**. In order to do so without the danger of pulling it too far back, you should include a slight pause at maximum backstroke and before the final power stroke. The pause will help prevent pulling the stick back too much or too little.

The upper body should move forward during the execution of the power stroke. The distance moved doesn't have to be far as long as it is quick and coordinated with arm movement. When some players break their back leg comes up off the floor and is kicked into the air. This is done to help stop the forward movement of the upper body.

As an example, assume arm stroke speed is 15 mph; if the upper body is moved forward at a speed of 3 mph (walking speed) the speed of the stick will be increased by 20 percent. This 20 percent increase in stick speed means a 44 percent increase in stick energy. This increase in energy will frequently translate into pocketing additional balls.

♦♦♦

BREAK STICK

Stick weight -- For many years it was thought that a heavy stick was much more effective than a light stick in breaking the balls. It seemed reasonable that a heavy stick would impart more energy to the cue ball than a light stick. As radar guns and other speed measuring devices became more available the heavy stick hypothesis began to erode. It is known that, as stick weight is increased, its speed is reduced, and at some point the reduction in speed will cause total stick energy to decline.

The optimum stick weight depends on the individual's physical stature and reflexes. Generally, the maximum stick velocity, generated by a small quick person, will diminish rapidly with increased stick weight. The stick velocity, of a large muscular person, will diminish less rapidly and therefore stick weight can be increased considerably before resulting in diminished returns. Most expert NINE-BALL players now break with a stick that weights about 19 ounces or slightly less.

A person that uses a long bridge distance may break better with a heavy stick than a person that uses a short bridge distance. The longer distance allows the heavy stick to accelerate longer before striking the cue ball.

Other stick characteristics – There are several other stick characteristics that determine the effectiveness of the break stick. They include stiffness, length, deflection, and type of wrap. Probability, the best way to experiment with different break sticks is to go to a pool hall that provides, or rents, two-piece cue sticks. When you find a stick that breaks exceptionally well—buy it.

◆ ◆ ◆

BREAK OVERVIEW

When breaking, it is important to observe where each ball goes. The problem is it's hard for the person that is breaking to observe every aspect of the break (because it happens so fast). Where did the 1-ball hit the cushion? Where did the wing ball hit? Where did the 9-ball go? If conditions allow, a video camera should be used to record your practice break shots for later analysis. If using a video camera is not feasible, try to have one or more friends watch and report where the various balls go.

Balls break differently from table to table, from one set of balls to another, and with changing room and ball conditions. If you're playing in a tournament, you should check to see how the balls are breaking just before your match (not a week before). During a match, always be sure to watch how the balls are breaking for your opponent; add that data to the observations of your own break. This way you will be gathering twice the data and your analysis will consequently be more reliable.

On a table where only games like 14-1 or ONE-POCKET are played, it is best not to put a reinforcement patch on the foot spot. The patch is not needed and will serve only to deflect the course of slow moving balls. On any table where a power break is used, it is always best to use a reinforcement patch. If the patch is not used an indentation is likely to develop in the cloth. An indentation in the cloth will deflect the movement of a ball much more than a patch will. And, if a hole or low spot develops, the 1-

45

ball will be lower than the other balls (when racked) and the balls won't break properly.

◆ ◆ ◆

CHAPTER 3

PUSH-OUT

T he *"push-out"* shot (also referred to as "roll-out" or "shoot-out") is unique to NINE-BALL so it will be examined in detail in this chapter.

To "push-out" means you can shoot the cue ball to any position on the table. Either player can use the push-out providing it is the first shot after the break shot. Some of the normal rules of fouling do not apply when the push-out is employed. It is not necessary to strike any object ball and no ball has to hit a cushion. You can pocket any ball on the table if you wish (all balls stay down except the 9-ball which is spotted).

A player *must* announce his\her intention of pushing-out before executing a push-out shot. If it is not announced, the shot is considered to be a regular shot and all the normal foul rules apply. After the push-out, the incoming player gets the option of taking the shot or giving it back to the first player.

The purpose of the push-out shot is to *limit* the luck factor in determining the winner of the game. For example the breaker may do an exceptional job of breaking (scattering and making balls) and still end up snookered behind another ball. The cue ball may be in such a bad position that a foul on the next shot is extremely likely. Having the push-out as an option changes the situation from <u>extreme bad luck</u> to <u>simple bad luck</u>. The person that elects to push-out is <u>always</u> at a disadvantage because the other player has the advantage of accepting or rejecting the next shot.

◆ ◆ ◆

PUSH OR SHOOT

When you decide to push-out you are immediately on the defensive. And keep in mind; you are favored to *lose* the exchange because your opponent will be given the *choice* of shooting or not shooting the shot you leave. Being the one that is able to make the decision gives the second shooter the advantage. Therefore, the push-out should be used mainly to avoid a foul, which would be an even greater disadvantage.

The objective of a push-out shot is to improve your situation from very bad to simply bad. If there is a chance of improving your situation, even a little, you should opt to push-out. Here are some questions to ask yourself before deciding whether or not to push-out:

1. What are the chances of executing a legal hit on the object ball? The smaller the chance of getting a good hit on the object ball, the more the situation calls for a push-out.
2. How devastating would a foul be? You must consider the consequence of not hitting the object

48

ball if you elect to shoot. If, for example, ball-in-hand would give your opponent a chance at a combination shot at the 9-ball, you should opt to push-out.

3. What kind of shot would you likely leave your opponent if you executed a good hit but fail to make a ball? In some cases a good hit may leave your opponent in a fairly safe situation and in other cases it would leave him/her with an easy shot.

4. If you push-out to a place where your opponent will have to shoot a safety, what are the chances of winning the ensuing safety battle? Thinking ahead one or more shots may unveil the proper course of action.

5. Would there be any advantage in moving another ball or balls? The push-out is not often thought of as an opportunity to move other balls but sometimes that can be an advantage. You may want to move the 9-ball away from a pocket even if you have a clear shot at the object ball. Or, you may want to move any ball(s) that would offer a combination on the 9-ball. You may want to create a cluster of balls. A cluster generally lengthens the game and the longer the game, the less effect the push-out (where you have the disadvantage) has on the outcome.

◆ ◆ ◆

CUE-BALL POSITION

Once you have decided to push-out you must decide where to push to.

49

Note: It is sometimes best to get the cue ball to its new destination by kicking off a cushion or caroming off another ball. Your opponent will be wondering what you were trying to do when he/she should be concentrating on his/her shot.

As a general rule the first thing to consider is to push to a place where you can shoot a safety if your opponent gives it back to you. This means a place where you can hit the object ball and still control where the cue ball ends up.

If your opponent is good at creating safeties you may want to leave a safety rather than a safety opportunity. That is, shoot to a place where the object ball cannot be hit directly with the cue ball. This will force your opponent to either shoot a jump, kick, some other low percentage shot, or give it back to you. Sometimes it is better to have to kick at a ball than to leave something better for your opponent.

In some situations it is best to push to a place where your opponent can make the object ball but can't get shape on the next ball, or, the ball after that.

If there is a cluster down the road, that you would rather have your opponent deal with, it may be good policy to leave your opponent a makeable shot. If there isn't a cluster, you could consider using your push shot to create one.

When the 9-ball is sitting in the jaws of a pocket it may be best to simply pocket the 9-ball while leaving the cue ball in the desired position. Since you are pushing-out, your opponent already has the advantage; you don't want to increase the advantage by leaving a possible combination on the 9-ball.

In order to make the best possible decision, as to where to leave the cue ball, you must take your own, as well as your opponent's, capabilities into consideration. Ask yourself the following questions:

1. Talent: Do you have any unique talents that your opponent does not have. If you can kick more accurately than your opponent, then push-out to a position that requires a kick shot. If you have a talent for two-rail kicks then leave a two-rail kick. If you can jump better than your opponent then try to leave a straight-in jump shot.

   Obviously having a unique talent can make a big difference when it comes to the push-out shot. This is a compelling reason to try to develop a unique talent that you can use for push-out situations. If you choose a specific type of shot, and practice it more than your competitors, you may win the push-out battle. For example, if you choose a curve shot for your specialty, practice it until you are sure you have practiced it twice as much as your opponent. Then, always push-out to a situation that requires a curve shot.

2. Physical advantage: Are you taller than your opponent? If you are then push-out to a position that you can reach (if the shot is given back to you) and your opponent can't. If your opponent is left handed, and you're not, push-out to a position that you can reach easily and your opponent can't. If your opponent is near sighted, leave a long shot. If

your opponent has short fingers leave a Chinese hook.

Of these physical differences handedness is probably the most important. If your opponent is opposite handed, _always_ give this first consideration when pushing out. Left-handed players have a decided advantage when it comes to pushing-out. This is because they have to deal with opposite handed players 95 percent of the time (right handers only 5 percent of the time). Because of this high frequency, left-handers will be able to apply this strategy more frequently than right-handed players.

3. _Psychological advantage_: Will your opponent shoot at anything? If yes, then leave an extremely difficult shot. Keep in mind; you want your opponent to accept the low percentage shots. Ideally, you want your opponent to shoot and miss leaving you better off than you were before you pushed.

Note: Some experts suggest that you strive to leave the cue ball in such a position that your opponent accepts the shot 50 percent of the time. The numbers work but the psychology doesn't. Letting your opponent make all the value judgments can't be good. And what if your opponent is making the wrong decisions; do you want his/her judgment to dictate your strategy?

◆ ◆ ◆

TAKE IT OR LEAVE IT

When your opponent pushes-out you must decide whether or not to take the shot. There are some questions you should ask yourself before deciding:

1. The first question is "can I make the object ball?" If it is a high percentage shot you should usually go for it. If it is a low percentage shot, you should continue to ask more questions.
2. Can you hit the object ball and leave an even more difficult shot for your opponent? If yes, go for it, if no; let your opponent take the harder shot.
3. What are the chances of executing a good safety? If the shot offers a good chance of executing a good safety, go for it.
4. The person that has the choice, more often than not, takes the shot. There are two main reasons for this. First, the person pushing usually wants to make the shot easy if it is given back and in doing so usually makes it too easy. And second, ego enters the equation; the player with the choice usually wants to accept the challenge. When it is your decision, ask yourself, "is it ego driving me to take the shot?"
5. Ask yourself what your opponent will do if you pass it back. For example, assume you can't bank very well but your opponent can. If you are left with a bank shot, are you going to pass it to your opponent knowing he/she will probably make it? In a case like this, it may be better for you to take

the bank shot even knowing that you probably won't make it.

6. Do you want to change the shooting sequence? There may be trouble balls down the road that you would rather have your opponent deal with. If so, shoot or don't shoot to establish the desired shooting sequence.

◆ ◆ ◆

PUSH-OUT EXAMPLES

Figure 3-1A shows a situation where the cue ball is pushed-out to a jump-shot situation. In this particular case hitting the 1-ball means winning the game because the 9-ball will go in on a combination. This push-out position is recommended if you are good at jump shots and your opponent isn't. Even if your opponent is an expert at jump shots, but is left handed, this would be an excellent position to leave the cue ball.

Figure 3-1B shows an excellent strategy for someone that is an expert at curve shots. The intervening ball is too far away to jump and still be sure of keeping the cue ball on the table; therefore, a curve shot is required. In recent years the jump shot has became so popular that many players have neglected to practice the curve shot. Therefore, expertise in curve shots would be an excellent specialty to have in your repertoire for push-out situations.

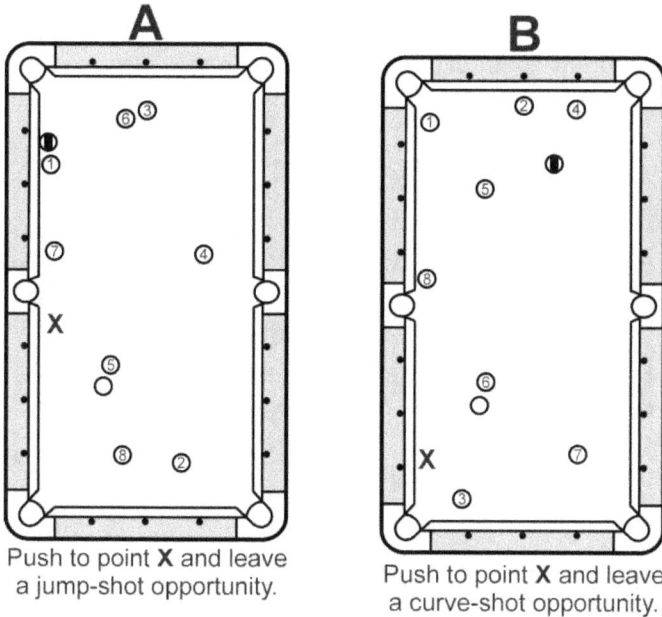

Push to point **X** and leave
a jump-shot opportunity.

Push to point **X** and leave
a curve-shot opportunity.

**FIGURE 3-1. Examples of where to leave the
cue ball when pushing out.**

If your eyesight is better than your opponent's,
leave a long thin cut shot. **Figure 3-2C** shows an
example of such a push-out shot. How long and how
thin depends on the disparity of visual acuity between
you and your opponent.

If you are tall and your opponent is short leave a
shot that requires a long stretch. **Figure 3-2D** shows
such an example. It is true that a shorter person could
use the mechanical bridge but, in doing so, accuracy
is usually reduced.

These example push shots demonstrate how
important it is to have a specialty that you can use to
advantage in pushing-out. Whenever you have to

55

push-out, leave a shot that requires the use of your particular specialty.

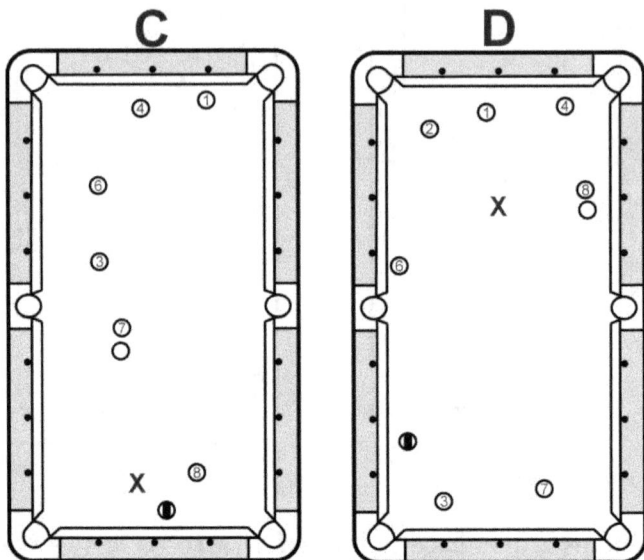

Push to point **X** and leave a long, thin cut shot.

Push to point **X** and leave a shot that's difficult to reach.

FIGURE 3-2. Examples of where to leave the cue ball when pushing out.

If you can bank better than your opponent leaving a long bank shot, as shown in **Figure 3-3E,** would be a good strategy. The appropriate distance left between the 1-ball and the cue ball will depend on your opponent's banking skill. If your opponent can't bank, leave the cue ball closer to the 1-ball.

If you can kick better than your opponent the strategy shown in **Figure 3-3F** would be appropriate. In this case it may be wise to bump into the 8-ball to insure stopping the cue ball where you intend.

Running the cue ball head-on into another ball is a good stopping technique, especially for shots, where the cue ball must be rolled a long distance.

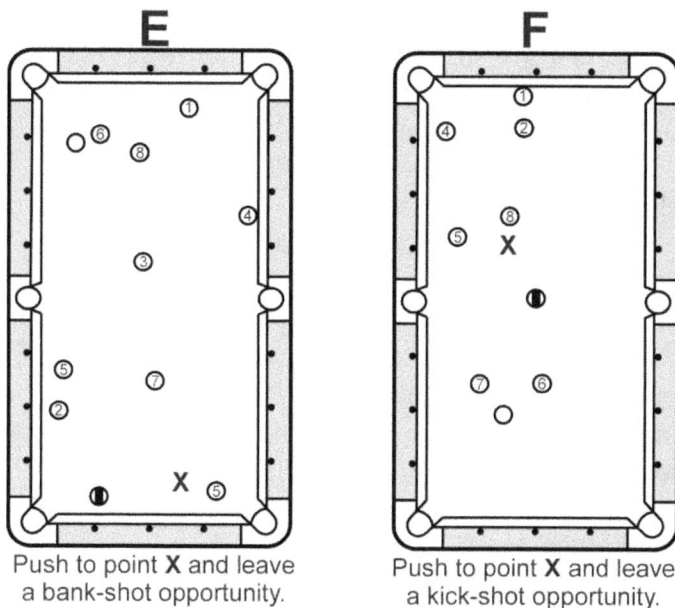

Push to point **X** and leave a bank-shot opportunity.

Push to point **X** and leave a kick-shot opportunity.

FIGURE 3-3. Examples of where to leave the cue ball when pushing out.

Be ruthless in planning your push-out shots. If your opponents are short, leave shots they can't reach. If your opponents have short pudgy fingers, make them shoot over a ball. If they can't see well leave them long, thin cut shots. If their handedness is different from yours, make them suffer as was done in **Figure 3-1A**. What do you do better than your opponent? Try to answer that question before the game starts.

♦ ♦ ♦

PUSH-OUT TESTS

Figure 3-4 shows two tables after the break shot. Assume you are the coach of several students of different stature and abilities. What would you advise your student players to do? Should they push-out or shoot? If so, where? The following discussion explores some of the possibilities.

Figure 3-4A:
The 1-ball can't be hit with certainty; therefore, a push-out is warranted. If you're tall and your opponent is short you can push-out toward the 7-ball leaving a thin cut into the corner pocket. It would be an awkward shot for a short person but a little easier for a tall person.

If you have good eyesight and your opponent doesn't you can push to the cushion near diamond **L**. How long you want to make the shot depends on the relative skills of both you and your opponent. When executing this shot try for a thin hit with maximum left english. If you don't hit the 1-ball going in, you will probably hit it coming off the cushion because of the english.

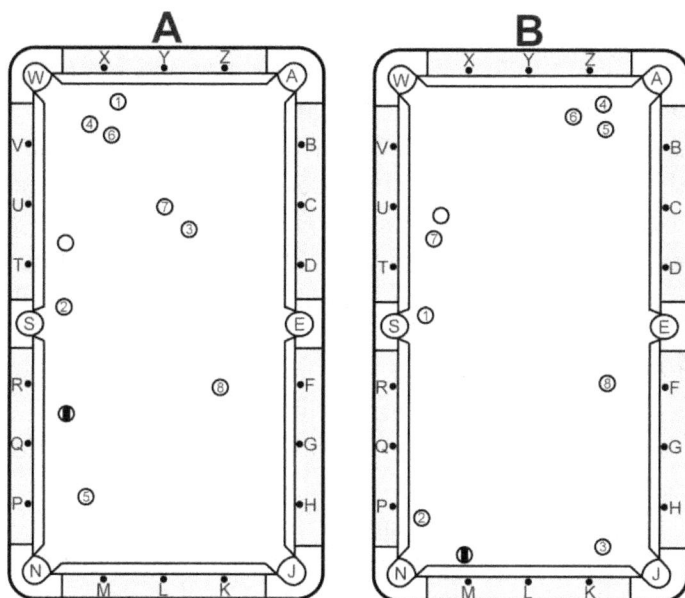

FIGURE 3-4. Where would you push to?

If you can kick better than your opponent you can push to point **T-Y** (coordinate point). From there you can kick to the cushion at diamond **C**. This shot offers an easy hit on the 1-ball because it is a "big ball." (Big target because you can hit the ball first or hit the cushion all the way to diamond **Y** and still hit the 1-ball.)

You can also push to a point by the cushion near diamond **F**. From there you can curve around the 3-ball into the 1-ball. Here again, you don't necessarily have to hit the 1-ball going in, you could hit the cushion first then go into the 1-ball. The english used to curve assures that the cue ball will come off the cushion angling toward the 1-ball.

59

Figure 3-4B:

Given this situation, it may be a good time to test an aggressive opponent. Shoot the cue ball to diamond **D**. Your opponent will take the shot because of the easy three-ball run. (Looking three balls ahead as any good player should.) But after shooting the 1-ball it becomes apparent that the 4-ball is almost impossible to hit. An aggressive shooter would probably shoot the 2-, and 3-ball with little chance of breaking out the 4-ball. Or, your opponent may shoot a safety at one of the balls (the safety would be a low percent shot because there are no easy balls to hide behind).

If your opponent smells the trap, and gives the push shot back to you, you can try to break out the 4-ball by shooting the 1-ball with top right english. The cue ball will probably hit the 5-, or 6-ball exposing the 4-ball. This is a fairly safe strategy because it is unlikely the cue ball will get behind any other ball which would prevent an easy shot at the 2-ball.

Figure 3-5C:

If you are tall enough, and can reach far enough, you can push the cue ball a few inches toward diamond **L**. This will allow a kick shot by shooting into the cushion at diamond **D** the kick is fairly easy because the 1-ball is a big ball.

Suppose you try the previous push and the cue-ball rolls too far and ends up near diamond **L**. This would leave a similar shot but at the opposite side rail (diamond **T**). Again this could be either a one or two rail kick.

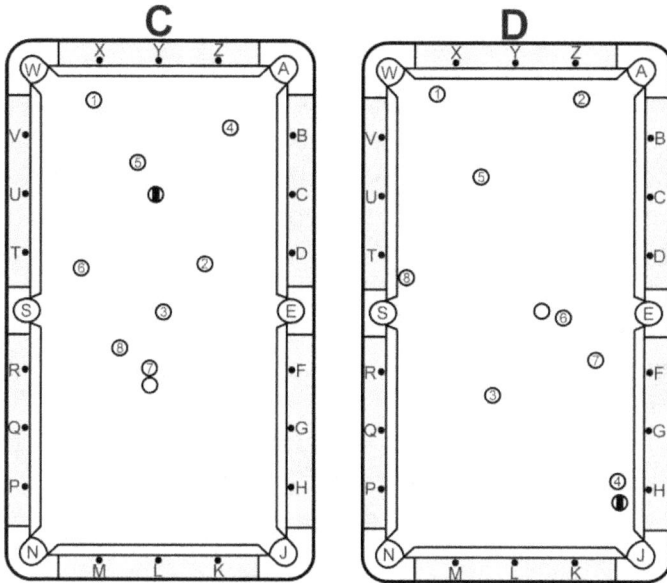

FIGURE 3-5. Where would you push to?

If you are right handed, and your opponent is left-handed, you can push-out toward diamond **R** leaving the 6-ball between the cue ball and 1-ball. The jump shot over the 6-ball would be much more difficult for your opponent than for you.

If you would rather leave a curve shot than a jump shot, you can push-out to the cushion near diamond **P**. From there you can curve around the 6-ball either to the right or left depending on the exact position of the cue ball.

Figure 3-5D:

The 4-, and 9-ball are lined up for an easy combination; so, whoever gets to the 4-ball first will most likely win the game. The 4- 9-ball combination could be shot or bumped from behind with a push if you think your opponent might get to it before you do.

If you're right handed, and your opponent is not, the cue ball can be pushed to the cushion near diamond **T**. But this move may backfire. Since the shot can't be reached, the opponent may opt for a kick shot into the cushion at diamond **C**. Since the 1-ball is slightly off the rail it could be made very easily. If the 1-ball goes in, the opponent will be favored to win this game because of the easy 4- 9-ball combination.

If your opponent has short fingers you may want to roll the cue ball up against the 3-ball.

◆ ◆ ◆

CHAPTER 4
SAFETIES

I n most games of pool, the majority of the shots are offensive; the shooter's prime objective is to pocket an object ball. However, there are situations in which pocketing a ball is not even a consideration; the only objective may be to leave a difficult shot for your opponent. These shots are called *safeties*. A safety is generally used when pocketing the object ball and/or getting shape on the next ball is very unlikely.

Safeties are a vital part of all pool games but are especially important in the game of NINE-BALL. The ultimate goal of a safety is to make the succeeding shot so difficult that the shooter is unable to make a good hit on the object ball and subsequently commits a foul. However, your opponent does not have to foul in order for your safety to be considered successful. **If your chance of winning is better after the safety than before, the safety was justified (good).**

In most respects, the safety shot is considered to be a defensive shot, however, this is not always the case. Every safety has some offensive as well as defensive elements. An example of a safety being used predominantly as an offensive shot would be an attempt to make the opponent foul three consecutive times (which would be a loss of game.).

♦♦♦

ETHICS OF SAFETIES

When shooting "barroom" or "social" EIGHT BALL executing a safety may not be considered ethical. In these circumstances safeties are sometimes referred to a "dirty pool" and are considered by some to be unsportsmanlike. In these settings an "honest effort" (to make a ball) is generally obligatory. However, a problem arises when the game gets a little more serious and "honest effort" starts to vary from player to player. In these circumstances some players may use safeties but disguise them as something else. Some may disguise their safeties better than others, but eventually; shades of *honest effort* will possibly lead to hostility. In NINE-BALL safeties are an accepted, ethical part of the game.

♦♦♦

THE POWER OF A SAFETY

Safeties are a deceptively powerful tool in winning games. A player that is not adept at executing safeties will be forced to attempt many low percentage shots. Shooting low percentage shots is a losing proposition. If you are even a little better than your opponent at executing safeties, you have a decided advantage.

64

While your opponent is taking chances shooting low percentage shots, you can be shooting high percentage safeties and winning games.

> Consider this: Imagine your opponent allowing you to skip all the difficult shots and just shoot the easy ones. Sounds too good to be true doesn't it? Well, that's the deal you get when you perfect your safety game.

♦♦♦

WHEN TO SHOOT A SAFETY

It is often repeated: "If you have a choice of shooting a hard safety or a hard shot you should always go for the shot." This rule of thumb works best when there are only a few balls left on the table. For example, if the 9-ball is the only ball left on the table you should follow the rule. However, when you are trying to decide on shooting a difficult shot at the 1-ball or playing safe, the rule may not be so hard and true. This is because the reward for making the 1-ball is much smaller than the reward for making a successful safety (especially true for average players).

When trying to determine whether or not to shoot a safety you must consider the long-term effects of your decision. When you go for an offensive shot, the object ball either goes into the pocket or it doesn't. The outcome of your decision can be considered black or white. When shooting a safety the result is always some shade of gray. That is, the value of the safety will range from very good to very bad.

The following are some situations where shooting a safety should be considered:

1. No pocket for the object ball.
2. Can't get shape on the next ball.
3. Bad cluster ahead.
4. If your opponent has two fouls, you must **always** consider shooting a safety. However, keep in mind that when your opponent has two fouls, you don't necessarily have to shoot a safety on the next shot, it can be one or two shots down the road.
5. Some players have a low frustration tolerance; in those cases it may be advantageous to shoot a safety just to break your opponent's rhythm.
6. A safety can sometimes be used to set up a combination shot at the 9-ball.

Figure 4-1 shows a situation that demonstrates the value of a safety at a crucial time. When confronted with the ball arrangement as shown, most players would shoot the 1-ball into the corner pocket. However, the shooter can elect to shoot a safety by positioning the 1-ball near the 9-ball while nestling the cue ball behind the 5-, 7-, 8-ball cluster. If the next player is unable to hit the 1-ball, and fouls, the game can be won by shooting an easy 1-9 combination.

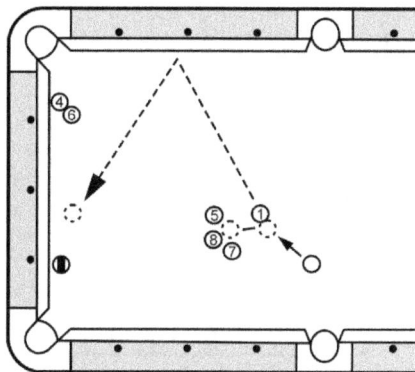

FIGURE 4-1. This safety should be considered. If the opponent fouls the game can be won with an easy combination.

Some shots have a built-in safety factor. That is, you can shoot for the object ball and if missed, your opponent will be left safe. These are usually referred to as **two-way** shots. **Figure 4-2** shows an example of a two-way shot. A bank shot on the 3-ball can be attempted. If shot with a stun stroke, the cue ball will stop behind the 5- and 6-ball. If the 3-ball is missed the shot can be considered a safety. If the 3-ball is pocketed, the run can continue because there is an easy shot at the 4-ball. This shot can actually be considered a three-way shot because if the first player misses the shot, and the next player fails to hit the 3-ball, there may be a chance of an easy 3- 9 combination.

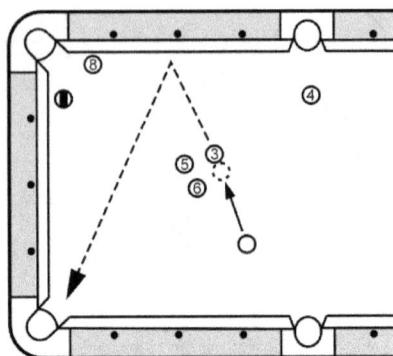

FIGURE 4-2. A two-way shot. If the 3-ball is missed, the shot could be considered a safety. If the 3-ball goes, the run can continue.

◆◆◆

ELEMENTS OF A SAFETY

Assign a priority -- When shooting a safety, the success of the shot depends on where both the cue ball and the object ball end up. At times the cue ball will go exactly where you want it to go but the object ball will go astray; at other times the cue ball will go astray. There are two main reasons why this happens. First, it is impossible to concentrate on both balls (object ball and cue ball) while you're executing the shot. And second, it may be a physically impossible to stop both balls where you intended them to stop.

You must decide which ball to concentrate on before you execute the shot. When shooting, concentrate on that particular ball's path. Simple physics will dictate where the other ball will stop. In that regard, here is a good rule to remember: **For any cut shot, you can control the rolling distance of one ball and only observe the other.** For example, if you want the cue ball to go to point **X** you have to hit it at a speed that will get it to point **X** regardless of where the object ball will go. If you want the object ball to go to point **Y** you have to strike it at a certain speed regardless of what you want the cue ball to do.

Physics of safeties -- In order to be successful at shooting safeties you must be able to accurately estimate how far both the object ball and cue ball will travel after they collide. The easiest way to estimate the relative travel of each ball is by relating it to the fullness of the hit.

For all but a very full hit on the object ball, the relative movement of the object ball is approximately equal to the fullness of the hit expressed as a percent. For example, if 50 percent of the object ball is hit (half ball hit), 50 percent of total movement (of both balls) will be done by the object ball and 50 percent by the cue ball. Another example: assume you are trying to hide the cue ball behind two other balls that are one foot away from the object ball. And, assume that you have to hit 75 percent of the object ball to make the cue ball go in the proper direction. How far will the object ball travel? At this cut angle, the ratio will be 75 to 25 or three to one. Therefore, for every one foot the cue-ball travels the object ball will travel three feet. If the cue ball is shot hard enough to go two feet, the object ball will travel six feet.

Hide cue ball or object ball -- Whether it is better to hide the object ball or the cue ball depends on the particular circumstances and the shooter's competence. Most players can predict the *direction* of the object ball more accurately than the direction of the cue ball after the collision. This is because the success of every shot depends on the direction precision of the object ball. On the other hand, most players can control the rolling *distance* of the cue ball better than the rolling distance of the object ball. This is because, in the normal course of play, the rolling distance of the cue ball must always be controlled in order to get shape for the next ball. The object ball stops in the pocket regardless of how fast it's going; therefore, that is not a consideration for most shots. When deciding whether to hide the object ball or the cue ball, you must decide if the shot is more direction sensitive or speed sensitive, then shoot accordingly. **All things being equal, it is usually better to hide the cue ball.**

Figure 4-3A shows an example of hiding the object ball. The 1-ball is cut thin so it strikes the cushion and rebounds to a position behind three other balls. The incoming player has to shoot a difficult kick shot just to hit the 1-ball. Given the same situation, a different safety could be executed. As shown in **Figure 4-3B**, the 1-ball is struck on the left side causing the cue ball to end up behind the clustered balls. Which safety to shoot depends on where the other ball (cue ball in **A** and 1-ball in **B**) will end up.

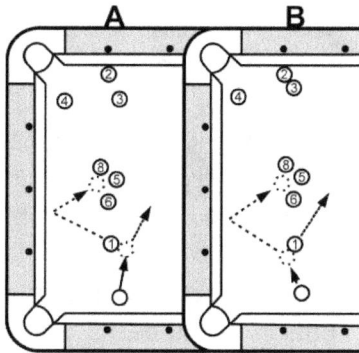

FIGURE 4-3. Either the 3-ball or the cue ball can be put into a difficult position.

Cue-ball position -- One of the safest places to leave the cue ball is frozen against another ball because it restricts the shooting direction to 180 degrees. If the next shot requires shooting away from the frozen ball, accuracy will be reduced because of having to use a precarious bridge.

The closer the cue ball is to the other ball, the more difficult it is for the next player. For example, if the cue ball is 24 inches away from the intervening ball the potential shooting arc is 350 degrees. As the cue ball is positioned closer to the obstructing ball, the potential shooting arc becomes progressively smaller. The *rate,* at which the shooting arc gets smaller, increases as the distance between the balls becomes shorter. For example, moving the cue ball from 24 inches away to 2.25 inches away (a ball diameter from the intervening ball) decreases the shooting arc by only 50 degrees. Moving the cue ball from 0.5 inch away (250 degree shooting arc) to 0.0 inches away (180 degree arc) decreases the shooting arc by 70 degrees. Obviously, it's important to get as close as possible to the object ball for the most effective defensive leave.

It is generally thought that the ideal position for the cue ball is directly between the cue ball and object ball as shown in **Figure 4-4A**. The 5-ball is directly between the cue ball and the 1-ball. This position is good but it is not ideal because it allows a kick at the 1-ball using either cushions **C** or **Y**. The ideal position, for the cue ball, is shown in **Figure 4-4B**. The intervening ball blocks the cue ball from being shot to the proper banking point on either cushion **C** or cushion **U**. Hitting the 1-ball by kicking to cushion **Y** is extremely difficult because of the long stretch and having to bridge over the intervening ball. In **Figure 4-C** there are balls blocking all the possible kicking cushions.

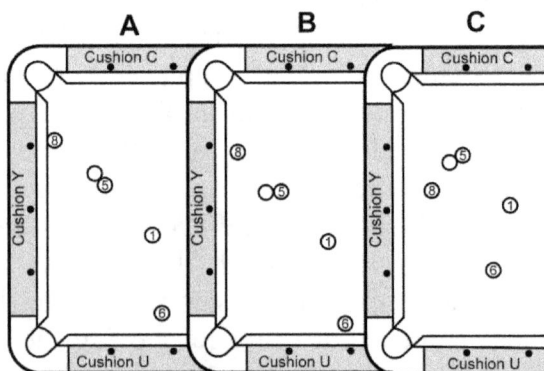

FIGURE 4-4. (A) The 1-ball can be hit with a kick to cushion C or Y. In (B) the object ball can only be hit with a difficult kick to cushion Y. In (C) the object ball can't be hit.

In most situations, having the intervening ball directly between the cue ball and object ball is not the most desired position. Always determine the potential kicking cushions before you execute the safety. Then, try to take away the best kicking cushion.

Leaving the cue ball near an intervening ball is obviously a good safety strategy. Leaving it near two or more balls restricts the potential shooting direction even more. Leaving it inside a cluster is even better.

Object-ball position -- Just as it is advantageous to leave the cue ball near an intervening ball, it is also advantageous to leave the object ball near an intervening ball. As with the cue ball, the closer the object ball is to the intervening ball the better. The more intervening balls the better because the cue ball may strike one of the nearby balls first which would be a foul.

It is usually advantageous to leave the cue ball near a cushion which may restrict the type of english the shooter can put on the cue ball. The opposite is true for the object ball. If the object ball is left near a cushion it sometimes presents a *big* target (usually referred to as a "big ball"). The 1-ball, in **Figure 4-5,** is a big target because it is near a cushion. The cue ball can either strike the ball directly or strike the cushion and rebound into the object ball.

Leaving the object ball in a corner presents an even bigger target; the 2-ball in **Figure 4-5** is an example. With the object ball in a corner, the cue ball can strike the object ball directly or strike either adjacent cushion and rebound into the object ball. All these options added together make an extremely large target.

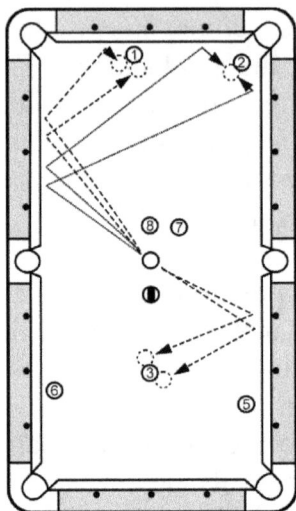

FIGURE 4-5. The 1-ball is a big target because it is near a cushion. The 2-ball is an even bigger target because it is near two cushions. The 3-ball is a small target because it is in the open.

The 3-ball in **Figure 4-5** presents the smallest target because it is out in the open. There are no cushions nearby to increase the effective size of the target.

◆ ◆ ◆

SAFETY STRATEGIES

There can be as many safety strategies as there are possible ball positions. However, there are some general strategies that are used often enough that they warrant individual scrutiny. The following are a few:

Picket fence defense -- The object ball can often be hidden behind two or more balls that form a "picket fence." As shown in **Figure 4-6**, the 1-ball is protected from the cue ball by the 8- and 9-ball. The 2-ball is protected by the 5-, 6-, and 7-ball. Keep in mind that any two balls can form a picket fence from somewhere on the table.

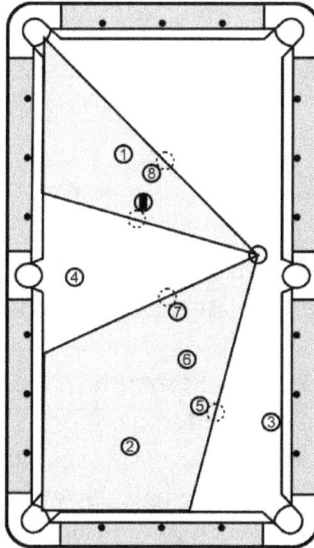

FIGURE 4-6. Two or more balls can act like a picket fence in protecting the object ball (1- and 2-ball) from being hit without using a kick shot.

The head-on shot -- The head-on shot into the object ball can be one of the best safety strategies. **Figure 4-7A** shows an example of hitting the object ball head-on. Pocketing the 1-ball would be difficult but a safety is very easy. A stun shot is used with enough speed so the 1-ball goes three rails and ends up at the other end of the table. **Figure 4-7B** shows the result of the shot. The 6-and 7-ball guard against an easy hit on the 1-ball.

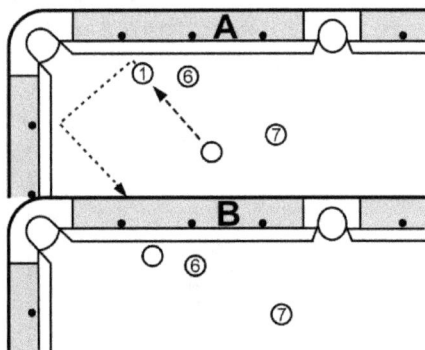

FIGURE 4-7. A stun shot can be used to stop the cue ball in a predictable position.

Nudging balls -- Sometimes, the blocking ball can be nudged into a better position; **Figure 4-8** shows such a case. The 8-ball is on the cushion and can be used as an interference ball. However, an interference ball offers the most blocking area when it is about a ball diameter away from the cushion. **Figure 4-8A** shows the cue-ball running into the 8-ball (after knocking the 1-ball down-table) nudging it off the cushion. Bumping the 8-ball does two things, it helps stop the cue ball and it moves the blocking ball into a

76

better position. **Figure 4-8B** shows the result of the shot.

In some cases the blocking ball may initially be more than a ball diameter from the cushion. In these cases it may be desirable to nudge the blocking ball closer to the cushion while leaving the cue ball on the cushion.

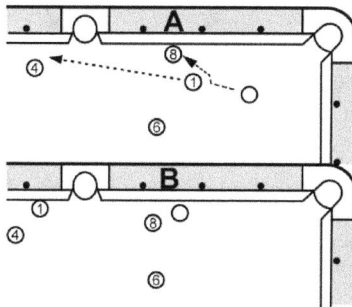

FIGURE 4-8. The cue ball should be made to run into the 8-ball so that it is nudged off the cushion and thus blocking a larger area.

Object-ball nudge -- Frequently, when there are only a few balls left on the table, it is not possible to hide the object ball or cue ball behind an intervening ball. In these cases it is usually best to leave the object ball and cue ball at opposite ends of the table. However, there are times when leaving the object ball and cue ball close together is the best strategy. When the object ball and cue ball are frozen together, or nearly so, it is usually difficult to make the object ball or even execute a return safety. **Figure 4-9** shows examples of this type of safety. In **Figure 4-9A** the object ball is gently shot head-on into the cushion.

The object ball strikes the cushion and rebounds directly back toward the cue ball. If the speed is just right they will end up frozen together. The better you're able to control the cue-ball's speed, the farther the cue ball can be from the object ball and still achieve a good result.

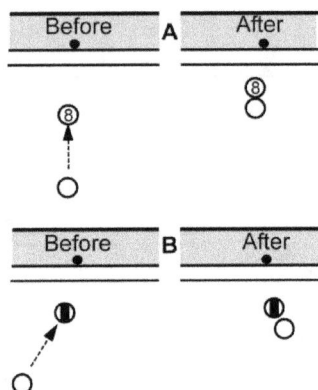

FIGURE 4-9. The object ball can be nudged into the cushion so it rebounds back and freezes to the cue ball.

This type of safety can be effective even if the two balls don't end up aligned perpendicular to the cushion. In fact, in many cases, it is more difficult for the opponent to shoot a return safety if the balls are not aligned perpendicular to the cushion.

Figure 4-9B shows a slightly different type of shot, the cue ball and object ball are not initially aligned perpendicular to the cushion. In this case the object ball must be struck slightly off-center in order for the two balls to end up close together. This shot may seem difficult if it has never been attempted.

However, with just a little practice it can be executed with great precision.

Stop-shot safety -- One thing that makes executing a safety difficult is the fact that the shooter must anticipate where **both** the object ball and cue ball will end up after the shot. Having to divide attention between the two balls tends to dilute attention. It would be much easier to concentrate on the path and travel distance of only one of the balls. This option is available if a stop shot is used. The cue ball will remain at the point of impact and the object ball will travel a very predictable route.

The first thing to consider when contemplating shooting a safety is: *can the object ball be struck head-on*, if so, what will its path be. Once the path of the object ball is known, you can determine if having it stop anywhere along this path will leave a difficult shot for your opponent.

Figure 4-10 shows a typical situation that calls for a safety. The 1-ball can't be made but it can be struck head-on by the cue ball. If struck head-on the 1-ball will take the path as shown. There are several safe zones along this path caused by intervening balls. The area between **"a"** and **"b"** is safe because of the 2-ball; the area between **"c"** and **"d"** is safe because of the 3-ball; and, the area between **"e"** and **"f"** is safe because of the 4-ball. Which of these safe areas is chosen depends on how easy it will be for the next player to successfully kick at the 1-ball.

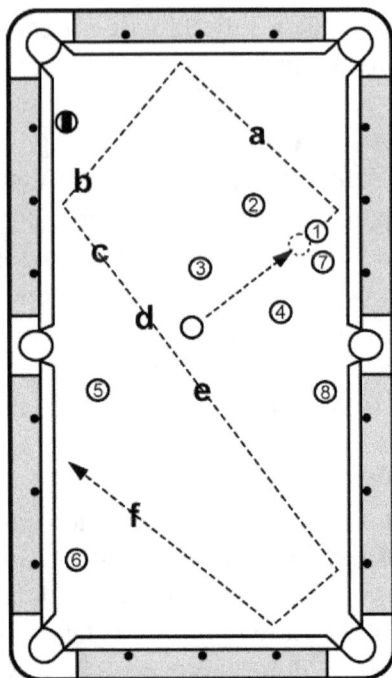

FIGURE 4-10. The "safe zones" along the path of the 1-ball are between "a" and "b"; "c" and "d"; and "e" and "f".

The stop-shot safety can also be used effectively when the direction of the object ball is altered by caroming off another ball. **Figure 4-11** shows such a shot. This type of safety is very elementary, but yet, is frequently overlooked. To avoid overlooking this type of easy safety, always ask yourself "What will happen it I strike the object ball head-on?"

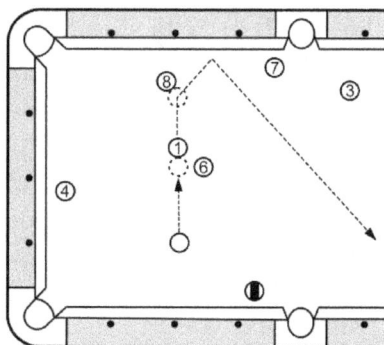

FIGURE 4-11. The stop shot can be used effectively when the direction of the object ball is changed by a carom off another ball.

Stop the object ball -- We already know that having to control the speed of only one of the two balls (cue ball or object ball) makes the safety much less difficult. By using a stop shot we can control very precisely where the cue ball will end up. Another option is to stop the object ball in a precise position so that the shooter can concentrate predominantly on the speed of the cue ball. This can be done if the object ball is made to run head-on into another ball. The object ball will stop (assuming it doesn't have much forward rotation) at a known position regardless of the speed of the cue ball.

Figure 4-12 shows an example of controlling the position of the object ball. The 1-ball could possibly be cut into the top left corner pocket. But, the 2-ball is in such a precarious position that making the 1-ball may not be a smart thing to do. The best thing to do, under these circumstances, is to execute a safety. The 1-ball can be shot head-on into the 8-ball. When the

1-ball hits the 8-ball it will stop. Since you know precisely where it's going to end up you can now concentrate on the speed of the cue ball. The cue ball can be shot slowly and stopped between **"a"** and **"b,"** or shot faster so that it stops between **"c"** and **"d,"** or at **"e."** Stopping at any one of these positions would be a good safety. If the cue-ball bumped the 2-ball into a makeable position it will be a great safety.

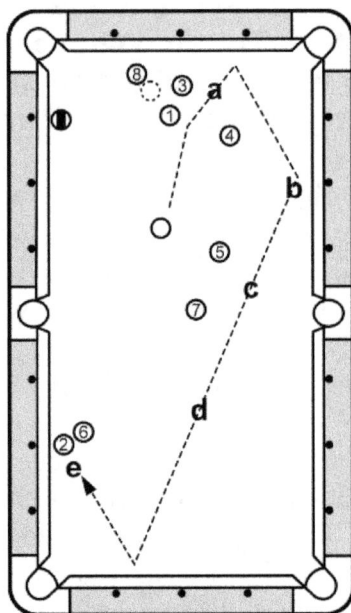

FIGURE 4-12. The "safe zones" along the path of the cue ball are between "a" and "b"; "c" and "d"; and at "e".

Leaving long -- There are many circumstances, especially when only a few balls remain, when it is impractical, or impossible, to leave an intervening ball between the cue ball and object ball. In these cases consideration should be given to leaving a long shot for your opponent.

The shot at the 7-ball in **Figure 4-13A** is an example of using the stop shot technique to put the balls on opposite ends of the table. The shot at the 5-ball in **Figure 4-13B** is another example of leaving the balls on opposite ends of the table. The 5-ball is shot into the 9-ball and stops. The cue-ball continues on to the other end of the table.

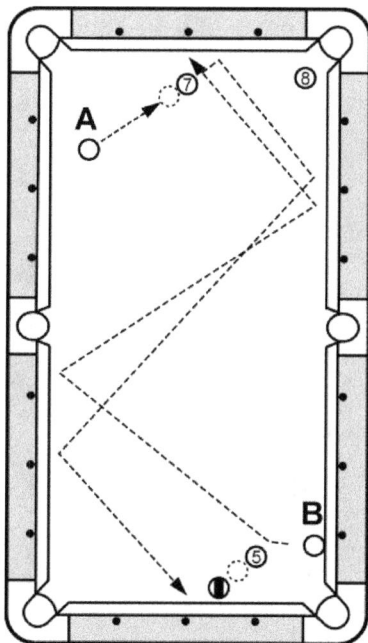

FIGURE 4-13. Two different types of safety shots. Move the cue ball to leave a long shot at the 5-ball and move the object ball to leave a long shot at the 7-ball.

If the object ball is more than about three inches off the cushion there may be a chance (depending on where the cue ball is) that it can be kicked to the other end of the table. When kicking head-on into an object ball that is near a cushion, the cue-ball stops; this leaves the cue ball near that cushion while the object ball is propelled toward the other end of the table.

Ball-in-hand -- There occasionally will be circumstances in which you will want to shoot a safety when you have ball-in-hand. It could be that you are trying to win by getting your opponent to foul on three consecutive shots or for numerous other reasons.

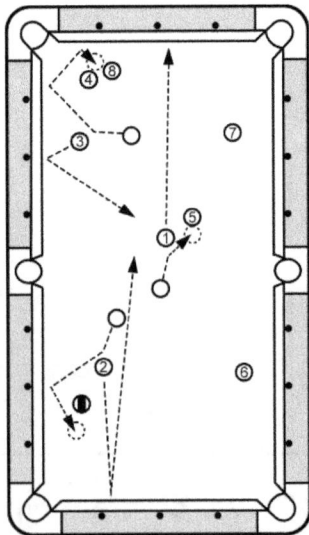

FIGURE 4-14. Three types of safeties that can be used when you have ball-in-hand.

Generally, when you have ball-in-hand, it is best to try to get the cue ball behind another ball or balls. **Figure 4-14** shows three of these types of shots. The safety on the 1-ball is the simplest. The 1-ball is shot to the cushion and the cue ball is parked behind an intervening ball. Most players think this shot is more difficult than it really is. The fact that you can place the cue ball in exactly the right position to begin with makes the shot easy. With a little practice the cue ball can be moved a considerable distance and still be stopped with great precision.

The safety on the 2-ball is similar but a cushion is used to position the cue ball behind an intervening ball. Two cushions are used for the safety on the 3-ball.

Game winning safeties – The game winning safety is the most often overlooked safety in the game of NINE-BALL. **Anytime the 9-ball is near a pocket, look for a game winning safety. Figure 4-15** shows one of these safeties. The 1-ball can easily be made in the corner pocket with open shots on the succeeding balls. A top professional could probably run the table nearly every time. For any other player, shooting a safety would be a much better option. If shot at the proper speed the 1-ball will end up near the foot cushion. If the opponent fouls it would leave an easy game winning combination shot on the 9-ball.

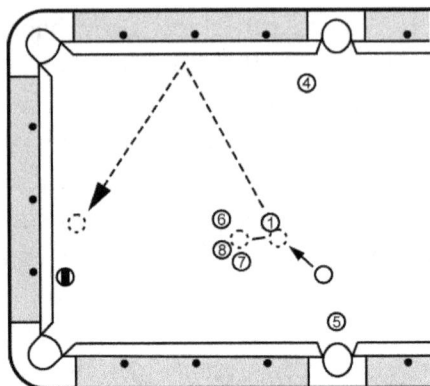

FIGURE 4-15. A potential game winning safety.

Safeties on the 9-ball -- There will be times when the only ball left on the table is the 9-ball; consequently, there are no other balls to hide behind. In this case the best strategy is to leave the 9-ball and the cue ball at opposite ends of the table. If that is not practical the shooter must be innovative in trying to leave difficult thin cut or bank shots. **Figure 4-16** shows several 9-ball safeties.

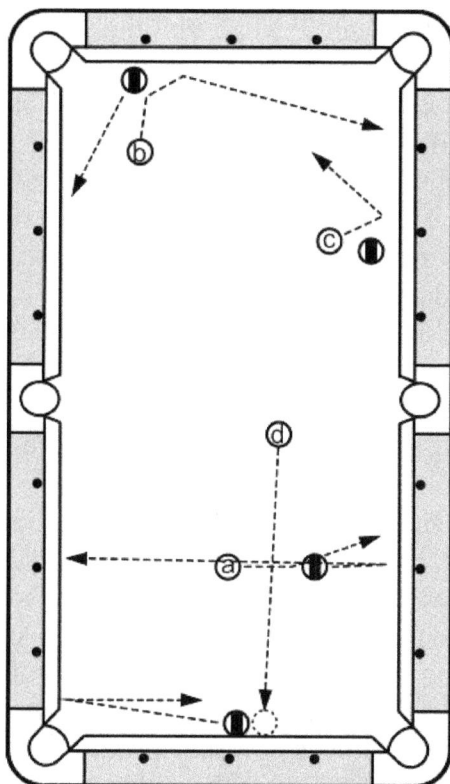

FIGURE 4-16. 9-ball safeties. (a) Right english with aim slightly left of center. (b) half-ball hit. (c) thin hit. (d) cushion first with right english.

In the shot shown with cue-ball **"a"** the 9-ball is hit slightly to the left of center with maximum right english. The cue ball goes to one side of the table and the 9-ball rebounds directly back to the other side of the table. This shot can also be executed the length of the table which is an even better safety.

In the shot with cue-ball **"b"** the 9-ball is struck a half-ball on the right side. The cue ball goes to the right side cushion and the 9-ball goes to the left side cushion. If this shot is struck a little harder, with left english, the 9-ball will go down to the other end of the table. The left english on the cue ball will cause it to slow down upon striking the first cushion and stay at that end of the table.

In the shot with cue-ball **"c"** the 9-ball is struck extremely thin. The 9-ball barely moves and the cue ball ends up near the end rail. The extremely thin hit is a very useful safety shot and, therefore, should be practiced and perfected.

In the shot with cue-ball **"d"** the cushion is struck first with maximum ball side english (right in this case). The cue-ball hits the 9-ball as it rebounds from the cushion. If struck perfectly the 9-ball will go into the corner pocket, if it misses the pocket it will rebound back into a safe area near the center of the end rail. If shot at the proper speed the cue ball will end up at the other end of the table.

♦ ♦ ♦

SAFETY EXERCISE

As an exercise, describe how you would shoot a safety at each ball in **Figure 4-17.** [Assume you're shooting some kind of safety game and not a game of NINE-BALL.] There is more than one way to execute a good safety on most of these balls. In the analyses that follow only one option is described.

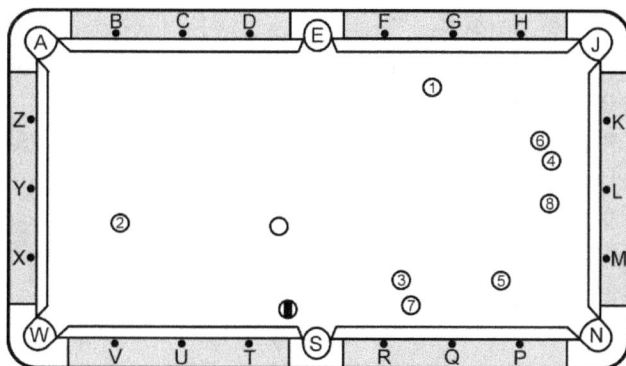

FIGURE 4-17. How would you shoot a safety at each of these balls?

1-ball -- The 1-ball can be struck head-on. After two cushions it will end up behind the 4- and 6-ball.

2-ball -- The 2-ball can be struck a little to the left of center using right english. The 2-ball will go to the end cushion and rebound back to diamond **L** or **M**.

3-ball -- The 3-ball can be struck a little to the right of center with a slow shot. The cue ball will go forward and stop behind the 7-ball.

4-ball -- The 4-ball can be struck a little to the right of center. The cue ball will end up behind the 8-ball.

5-ball -- The 5-ball can be struck on the left side sending it toward **P** then **L**. Hopefully, it will stop behind the 8-ball or the 4- 6-ball cluster.

6-ball -- The 6-ball can be struck nearly head-on using stop english. The 6-ball will go in and out of the corner and hit the third cushion near **U** ending up near diamond **X** or **Y**.

7-ball -- The cue ball can be shot at **R** and rebounded into the 7-ball. The cue ball will stay at the collision point and the 7-ball will get involved with the balls near the end of the table.

8-ball -- The 8-ball can be nudged behind the 4- and 6-ball.

9-ball -- The cue ball can be slow rolled into the 9-ball so that the 9-ball barely makes it to the cushion. The two balls will be left frozen together.

◆◆◆

RESPONSE TO SAFETIES

The judicious use of safeties can obviously be an effective weapon in NINE-BALL strategy. Your opponent will probably also come to this realization and use safeties against you. Therefore, you must be prepared to respond to a safety.

Hitting the object ball -- Assume your opponent has executed a good safety; your main concern is to execute a good hit thereby avoiding a foul. If a good hit is easy then consideration should be given to adding additional elements to the shot. The following are some elements that should be considered:

1. In some cases there are several directions from which you can kick at the object ball. Consideration must be given to using the shot that is most likely to pocket the object ball. If just hitting the ball is the objective, shoot the kick shot that presents the biggest target (big ball).

2. In some cases hitting the object ball from a particular direction will offer a greater chance of leaving a difficult shot, or possibly even a safety, for your opponent. You may even consider taking a harder shot at hitting the object ball if there is greater reward if you happen to succeed in hitting it.

3. If hitting the object ball requires a difficult kick, or some other equally difficult shot, you should aim for the center of the object ball. However, if you can hit the object ball fairly easily, consideration should be given to hitting it off center if there is an advantage to be gained.

4. Even when you are forced to aim for a center-ball hit on the object ball, you still have another option. That option is *speed*. When shooting a precarious kick or some other low percentage shot, most players tend to shoot at their personal "comfort speed". This is usually not the best strategy. For most safety responses, a little difference in speed will drastically alter the results of the shot. Always visualize where you want the balls to end up and use the speed necessary to accomplish that result.

5. The slow-nudge shot is the most predictable and should be used in preference to a faster speed shot. As speed is increased the end result becomes less and less predictable. However, there are circumstances when you should blast away at the object ball and hope for something

good to happen. This is usually the case when your best analytical judgment tells you that nothing good can happen when shooting at a reasonable speed.

Can't hit object ball -- If a good hit on the object ball is extremely difficult or impossible, the next best option should be considered. Generally this option entails accepting the foul and doing whatever is required to prevent your opponent from running out. Several of these options are listed:

1. Roll another ball between the object ball and the easiest pocket. Taking away the easiest pocket may not stop your opponent's run, but it will make it more difficult.
2. Create a difficult cluster which may stop your opponent's run. In **Figure 4-3A** the 2- and 3-ball are in the open where each can be made. In **Figure 4-3B** the 2-ball has been moved next to the 3-ball creating a difficult cluster.
3. Disturb any potentially easy 9-ball combinations. This may require moving or making the 9-ball, or, just moving other balls close to the 9-ball.
4. If the object ball is nestled in a cluster, you must do something to break up the cluster to prevent your opponent from using ball-in-hand to shoot another safety. This could potentially lead to a three-foul loss of game.

◆ ◆ ◆

SAFETY ESCAPES

Players that expect to be successful at escaping safeties must be competent at several specialty shots. The specialty shots must be practiced and perfected. Some of these specialty shots are:

One-rail kick: The kick shot is *the* most effective shot in getting out of a safety. The kick shot must be practiced at different speeds and with the use of various types of english. It is not good enough just to be able to kick into the object ball; you must strive to be able to propel the object ball in a desired direction.

Two-rail kick: If the object ball can't be struck using a one-rail kick, it can generally be struck using a two-rail kick. These shots are especially valuable in being able to get behind the object ball when it is near an end cushion. When hitting the object ball from behind the cue ball stops at the point of collision. This means you have a good idea of where the cue ball will end up; with this knowledge you can plan a more precise leave.

Curve shot: Since the rise in the popularity of the jump shot the curve shot has been overlooked and neglected. However, it remains one of the best weapons in getting around a distant intervening ball.

Curve-kick shot: The curve can be combined with the kick to increase the effectiveness of both. Assume you have to get around the left side of an intervening ball and go as far to the right as possible after it rebounds off the cushion. By applying right english the cue ball will curve to the right (helping the situation) and when it hits a cushion it goes even farther to the right (additional help). In essence, the curve and english compliment each other.

Kick-curve shot: If top or bottom english is used when striking a cushion at an angle, the cue ball can be made to curve slightly after it rebounds from a cushion.

Jump: At certain distances the jump shot is still the best safety escape tool.

Kick-jump: With practice, the cue ball can be made to jump back off a cushion and over an obstructing ball with the use of top english.

◆◆◆

SAFETY OVERVIEW

One question you must ask yourself when contemplating shooting a safety is; will it improve your chance of winning the game. You must consider both the physical and psychological effects of shooting a safety. Some opponents become frustrated when confronted with a flurry of safeties and their game falls apart. In some situations, shooting a safety when you have an easy shot may further confound your opponent.

Many players don't spend much time practicing safeties. This is a big mistake because if you are even a few percent better at executing safeties you have a tremendous advantage. Let your opponent take chances shooting low percentage shots while you're shooting high percentage safeties.

◆◆◆

CHAPTER 5

BALL-IN-HAND

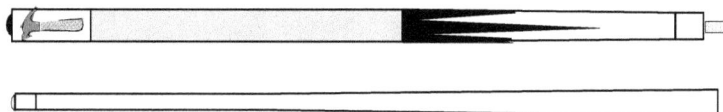

M‍any pool players don't even know what ball-in-hand means because it is not commonly used in barroom EIGHT-BALL. *Ball-in-hand* means that the shooter can place the cue ball (by hand) any place on the table for the next shot. A player gets ball-in-hand as a result of a foul committed by the other player.

◆◆◆

FOULS

In order to get ball-in-hand your opponent must commit a foul. Generally, good sportsmanship dictates that the shooter tells the opponent when a foul has been committed. However, at times the shooter may not even be aware that a foul was committed (like when a ball fails to strike a cushion). On these occasions it is the responsibility of the opponent to detect and call the foul. If, when your opponent is shooting, you see that the shot may result in a foul, it is your responsibility to request a referee or some other unbiased observer to monitor the shot.

♦ ♦ ♦

THREE-FOUL WIN

Three consecutive fouls constitutes a loss of game (dictated by the rules). A player usually does not get three consecutive fouls without deliberate action by the other player. However, getting your opponent to foul three times in a row is not an easy task. And, the more skilled the players are the rarer the three-foul win is. When your opponent has one foul you should consider going for the three fouls. When your opponent has two fouls you should **seriously** consider going for the three fouls.

When there is a cluster of balls on the table it is harder to win by running the table. If you can't run the table it is advisable to end your inning with a safety. If your safety is successful, and your opponent fouls, you are on the path for a three foul win.

Clusters are not the only reason to consider going for a three-foul win. Any situation that makes a run difficult should be sufficient reason to consider going for a safety and consequent three fouls. For example, if a run requires moving the cue ball back and forth the length of the table a three foul should be considered. Having to travel a great distance between shots increases the chance of an error, which in turn reduces the chance of a run. **Figure 5-1** shows such a situation. In this case, the 1-ball should be shot up-table leaving the cue ball behind the 8-ball. If the opponent fouls you can shoot the 1-ball back down table while leaving the cue ball behind the 9-ball. If your opponent fouls again, you are only one foul away from a win.

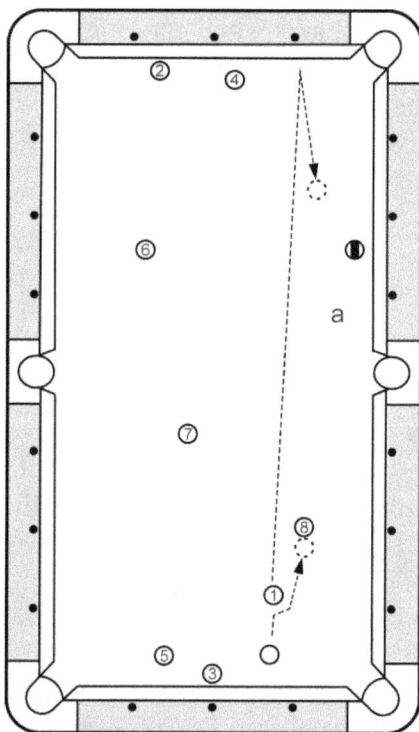

FIGURE 5-1. When a run requires going back and forth from one end of the table to the other for shape, trying for a three-foul win should be considered.

Be sure to tell your opponent that he/she has two fouls immediately after the second foul (the rules say you must). If the third foul occurs, and you haven't declared the two fouls, you won't get the three-foul win.

Pay attention to the number of fouls your opponent has. Consecutive fouls are usually observed and registered without a problem. However, fouls can easily be overlooked when one player makes a few balls between consecutive fouls by the other player. Or, by unexpected fouls caused by scratches or miscues. Even professional players occasionally fail to recognize a three foul.

◆ ◆ ◆

SAFETIES

A player normally resorts to a safety when there is little or no chance of making the object ball. When you have ball-in-hand you can usually make the object ball so there isn't the same motivation for the safety.

Shooting a safety, with ball-in-hand, is usually an attempt at getting the opponent to three-foul. However, in many situations a safety can be used to perform other functions such as nudging another ball loose, breaking up clusters, clearing shooting lanes, setting up combinations, or some other function. Having ball-in-hand makes these tasks easier because you have absolute control over the cue-ball position for the shot.

◆ ◆ ◆

INTENTIONAL FOULS

On some rare occasions it may be best to shoot an intentional foul when you are given ball-in-hand. This may occur when the object ball is in a cluster of balls as shown in **Figure 5-2**. The 2-ball can't be made even with ball-in-hand so there is no point in shooting at it. The best thing to do is make it so difficult that your opponent can't hit the object ball. This can be done by rolling the 3-ball into the cluster as shown. In doing so, you are assured that your opponent will have to foul again (two fouls). Your opponent fouled first so trading another foul will give you the win.

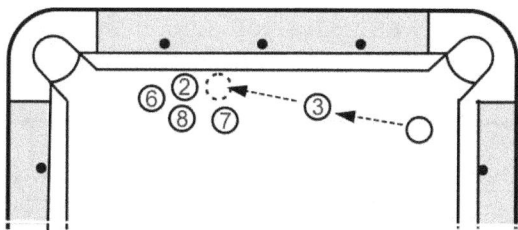

FIGURE 5-2. If you have ball-in-hand, it may be advisable to shoot an intentional foul.

If your opponent moves a ball away from the cluster on the next shot, you can move it back on your next shot. The only thing your opponent can logically do (while committing the second foul) is to try to separate as many of the clustered balls as possible. The more clustered balls that are left in the area, the easier it will be for you to shoot another successful intentional foul.

Figure 5-3 shows another situation where an intentional foul is warranted. The only way the 7-ball can be hit would be to shoot a long kick shot to the other end cushion. Even if you are successful in hitting the 7-ball nothing good will come of it; your opponent will probably get left with some sort of shot at the 7-ball. A better strategy would be to shoot the 9-ball into the corner pocket thereby committing a foul and giving your opponent ball-in-hand. Even with ball-in-hand, your opponent can't do much with the 7-ball. If your opponent shoots and breaks out the 7-ball, you will probably be in a better situation than you were originally. If your opponent avoids shooting by intentionally fouling, you will have ball-in-hand. Ball-in-hand won't give you a good shot but you will be much better off than you were originally.

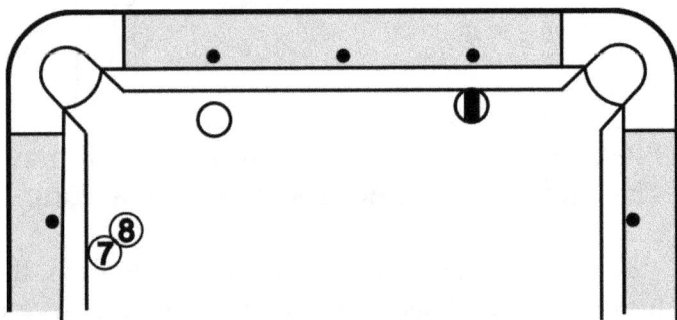

FIGURE 5-3. In this situation it may be best to shoot an intentional foul.

◆ ◆ ◆

9-BALL COMBINATIONS

Combination shots at the 9-ball, like any other combination shot, are usually fairly difficult. But, with ball-in-hand, you are able to position the cue ball within millimeters of the optimum position; this significantly decreases the difficulty of combination shots. Therefore, when you are given ball-in-hand you should always look for a possible combination shot (or carom shot) at the 9-ball.

Ball-in-hand combination shots, at the 9-ball, are most common right after the break shot. There are several reasons for this: First, scratches on the break are common. Therefore, getting ball-in-hand after the break occurs relatively frequently. Second, the 9-ball is frequently left near one of the corner pockets at the foot of the table, making for an inviting target. And third, there are a lot of balls on the table making a run challenging. Therefore, the advisability of going for the combination is greatest at this point in the game.

Several possible ball-in-hand combination shots are shown in **Figure 5-4**. They are:

1-ball: 9-ball combination carom shot.

2-ball: Combination bank into the 9-ball.

3-ball: Kick carom into the side pocket.

4-ball: Carom on the 9-ball into the side pocket.

5-ball: 9-ball combination bank into the corner pocket.

6-ball: Draw the cue ball into the 9-ball.

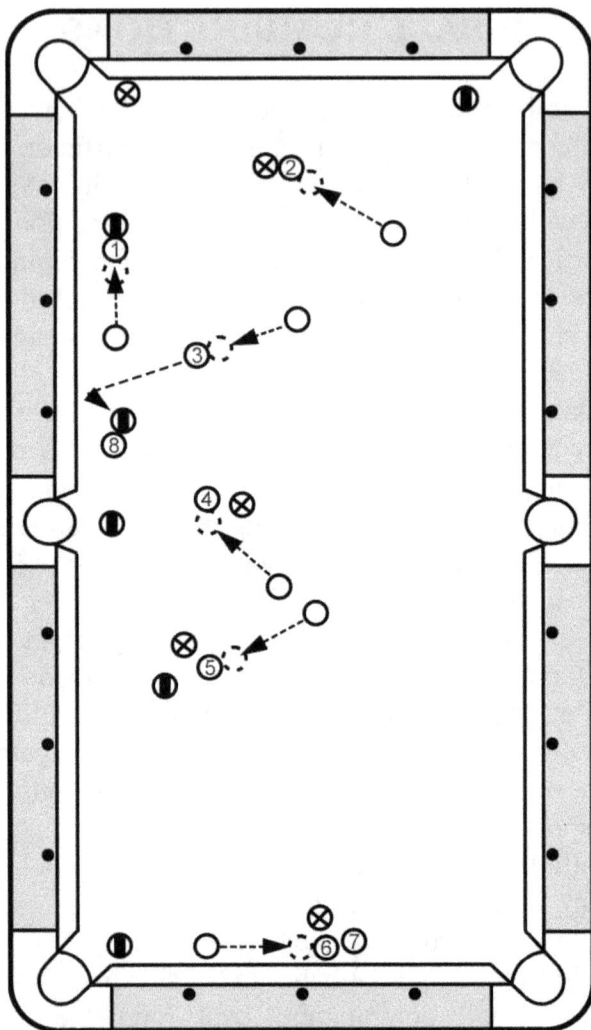

FIGURE 5-4. Examples of several 9-ball combination shots available with ball-in-hand.

Easy 9-ball combination shots are recognized and executed by most NINE-BALL players. However, many of the more unusual shots at the 9-ball (as shown in **Figure 5-4**) go unnoticed by many players. This is because they require perfect shape to be a viable shot and perfect shape is so seldom gotten that the shots are summarily dismissed. But, with ball-in-hand, perfect shape can be gotten every time, which makes these shots practical.

◆◆◆

TWO-WAY SHOTS

A two-way shot is a shot in which an attempt is made to pocket the object ball and at the same time, leave the cue ball safe if it is missed and with shape on the next ball if it is made. The purpose of the two-way shot is to be able to take a chance on a low percentage shot while still playing safe.

Two-way shots aren't used much during the normal course of play because they require a unique positioning of the object ball, cue ball, and next ball. With ball-in-hand these unique conditions are met much more frequently. Therefore, two-way shots, with ball-in-hand, can be useful and viable shots.

With ball-in-hand, the two-way shot is most commonly used on 9-ball combinations in the early part of the game. Having ball-in-hand, you can attempt combination shots on the 9-ball that would normally be too risky. **Figure 5-5** shows some two-way shots on the 9-ball made easy with ball-in-hand.

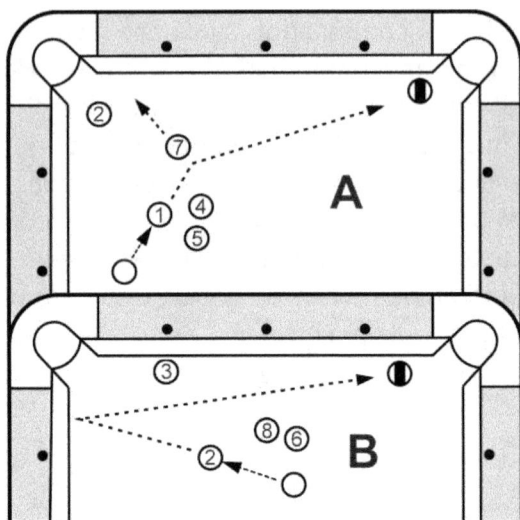

FIGURE 5-5. Two viable two-way stop shots at the 9-ball.

In **Figure 5-5A** the cue ball is positioned so that a head-on stun shot on the 1-ball will cause the 1-ball to carom off the 7-ball and pocket the 9-ball in the corner pocket. The cue ball stays behind the 4- and 5-ball so that, in case the 9-ball is missed, the opponent won't have an easy shot.

In **Figure 5-5B** the cue ball is positioned so that a head-on stun shot on the 2-ball will cause it to bank off the side cushion and into the 9-ball putting it into the corner pocket. The cue-ball stays behind the 6- and 8-ball so that, in case the 9-ball is missed, the opponent won't have a shot at the 2-ball.

♦ ♦ ♦

CUE-BALL PLACEMENT

The most common ball-in-hand mistake made by inexperienced players is placing the cue ball too close to the object ball (to make aiming easy). Placing the cue ball too close to the object ball does not allow for a normal follow through. When the follow through is restricted (for fear of double hitting the cue ball) aim and speed accuracy suffer.

As a result of experience, pool players become conditioned to do things the same way every time. Shooting the object ball into the nearest pocket is an example. When given ball-in-hand the first thing the player thinks about is shooting the object ball into the nearest pocket. But this conditioning is unduly restrictive. With ball-in-hand you can get perfect shape every time so this allows the shooter to select a little harder target if it will provide better shape for the next shot.

Any time you get ball-in-hand, look the table over for problem balls. If there are clusters that need to be broken up or balls that need to be bumped away from the cushion, now is the time to consider doing it. With ball-in-hand you get perfect cue-ball placement to do all these dirty little jobs.

◆ ◆ ◆

BALL-IN-HAND OVERVIEW

Ball-in-hand allows you to be creative in your shot selection. With ball-in-hand you can go for shots and shape that you would not normally consider. For example, you may go for more safeties because they are easier when you have ball-in-hand. You may want to get your opponent to three-foul just because it is easier with ball-in-hand. Attempts can be made at pocketing the 9-ball, out of order, often with impunity.

Some argue that the advantage of ball-in-hand is small for expert players. The philosophy is that they are so good at getting shape that every shot is like having ball-in-hand. The amateur player rarely gets perfect shape so ball-in-hand offers a huge immediate advantage. In either case the advantage of ball-in-hand lasts for only one or two shots so it should be made to pay regardless of skill level.

◆◆◆

CHAPTER 6
STRATEGY

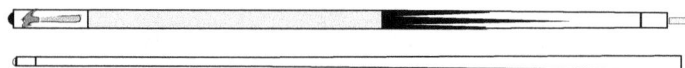

Strategy, as used here, is planning and maneuvering to one's best advantage. The quality of one's strategy determines the ultimate difficulty of the individual shots. Good strategy makes any given sequence of shots easier. To reduce the difficulty of a series of individual shots, one need only increase the quality of strategy.

In games like EIGHT-BALL selecting the sequence in which the balls should be pocketed is the most critical aspect of strategy. In the game of NINE-BALL the rules dictate the ball sequence so the most critical aspect of strategy is selecting a pocket for the ball and a means of getting shape to make it in that pocket. In this chapter selecting a shot refers to selecting a pocket and getting shape for that pocket.

◆ ◆ ◆

STRATEGY FLEXIBILITY

Good players usually have a plan for every ball before shooting the first shot. This may be good but

107

the plan must not be too ridged. The problem is, strategy errors are cumulative. That is, if you get a little out of shape on first ball you will probably get more out of shape on the next ball. The errors snowball until the original plan must be changed or modified.

Just because a plan does not always work as expected does not mean that all planning should be abandoned. Even a weak plan is better than no plan at all. Consider an automobile trip from California to New York as an analogy. If you have no plan at all you might as well stay home because you will never get to your destination. If you have the rudiments of a plan, for example, "drive east" you at least have some chance of getting to your destination. If you have the entire route plotted on a road map your chance of success is even better. But even though you have the route plotted very carefully you may have to make detours around road repairs. When you come to a detour you can't simply stop in despair and you can't trudge through the road repair. You must get out your map and plot a new course around the obstacle.

The same principals apply to pool; devise a detailed course of action but be ready and willing to change the plan if the need arises.

◆ ◆ ◆

PACE OF GAME

When you get to the table, especially after watching your opponent shoot for a long time, you are cold. Your shooting muscles are not able to perform at 100 percent immediately after being dormant for a period of time. In addition, your mind will not function at 100 percent immediately after the dormancy. After shooting a few shots everything gets back in working order, but what can you do to improve those first few shots?

The first thing you must do is <u>slow things down</u>. The first two or three shots should take nearly twice as long as your normal shooting pace. After the first few shots you can gradually speed up to your normal tempo. During the time you are shooting slowly you should be exercising your mind and muscles.

The best way of getting your mind and muscles back into the game is to simulate a few shots. Aim at the object ball as though you were going to shoot it directly into the pocket without using a cue ball. Take a few warm-up strokes at it. Then go over to where you expect the cue ball to end up; get down and take a few more strokes simulating your second shot. All this thinking and stroking will accelerate the process of getting your mind and muscles back to 100 percent without missing a shot.

♦ ♦ ♦

PROBABILITIES

Whether it is done consciously or otherwise the mind must go through a mathematical process each time a shot, or sequence of shots, is evaluated. Strategy must be based on the probability of something happening if a certain action is taken. Probability is not certainty, what is probable may not happen; what is improbable may happen. Your strategy selection can be perfect and you may still lose games that you should have won and vice versa.

Every pool player must assess probabilities based on their own personal experience and observations. The database is not stored in the form of easily accessible records; it is stored in the mind of the individual. Being stored in the mind, it is subject to all the frailties of the mind's storage and retrieval system. Another problem is the many variables associated with the stored data. For example, when even one variable is changed (like table speed or cue-ball weight) the database becomes less accurate and the decisions made based on these data become less reliable.

In order to determine which pocket to shoot for, and how to get shape for the next shot, the mind must estimate the probabilities associated with each and every course of action. Your mind must take into consideration your own personal skills. Players of different skill levels or players that have different skills should select different shots and shape. Usually, we are not even aware of the processes that our mind must go through in planning a sequence of shots. Aware of it or not, the mind must systematically process the visual data. The more accurately it processes these data, the better we play pool.

The selection of shots (plan) should be such that it affords the greatest chance of winning the game. As an exercise, let's assume a situation where there are only three balls left on the table: Which strategy scenario would be better?

A) Shoot a conservative 50 percent shot at each ball.

B) Select a more difficult 10 percent shot at the first ball so that there would be an easy 70 percent shot at the remaining two balls. The mathematical chance of running the table in scenario "**A**" is 12.5 percent and in "**B**" is 4.9 percent. Obviously, scenario "**A**" is more than twice as good as scenario "**B**." Scenario "**B**" is undesirable because of the one difficult 10 percent shot (even though shooting it increases the probability of making the other shots). The lesson in this example is to **avoid the extremely difficult shots** whenever possible. You are much better off selecting a uniformly conservative strategy than a roller-coaster type of strategy.

How do you avoid the difficult shots? Try not to include any difficult shots in your strategy plan but if that fails, shoot a safety rather than shoot the difficult shots. A strategy that incorporates a planned safety is much better than a strategy that incorporates a planned difficult shot.

When calculating probabilities be sure to keep in mind that missing a shot is not the same as losing the game. When you miss a shot there is still an X percent chance that your opponent will also miss and you will get another chance at winning the game. For example, assume two players (**A** and **B**) each make a ball on 50 percent of their shots. Assume the 9-ball is the only ball left on the table and player "**A**" shoots first. What is the chance that player "**A**" will win the game? There is a 50 percent chance that he will win with the first shot, but if he doesn't, there is a 50 percent chance that he will get to shoot again and will again have a 50 percent chance of making the ball and winning the game. In the end, after adding all of player **"A's"** chances, it turns out he has a 67 percent chance of winning the game.

Note: If player **"B"** made a ball 100 percent of the time (never misses) he would still have only a 50 percent chance of winning the game.

◆ ◆ ◆

STRATEGY VARIABLES

Appropriate strategy may vary somewhat depending on variables like the player's skill level, equipment, opponent, score, and mental aspects.

The strategy of a novice is usually limited to selecting a pocket for the object ball. As the player's ability increases, strategy becomes progressively more important and the objective broadens to include making all the balls and ultimately to winning the game.

Equipment -- Like people, most tables have their own personalities. Even tables of the same manufacturer, make, and model may play slightly differently. Table variables include type and stretch of cloth, pocket shimming, height and tightness of the rails, etc. The longer you play on a table the more

112

familiar you become with its unique characteristics; you must adjust your strategy to allow for these characteristics. For example, you should avoid bank shots if the cushions are unpredictable or avoid slow shots if the table isn't level. Jump shots don't work well on some tables, in these cases a curve or kick shot should be considered.

The cue ball can be bigger or smaller and weigh more or less than the object balls. Whether to go forward or backward for shape may be dictated by the size and weight of the cue ball. How clean or dirty the balls are may dictate how much they throw and that may also affect your strategy.

Opponent -- Your opponent's weaknesses may influence your strategy. For example, if your opponent gets frustrated easily you may want to shoot more safeties than you normally would. If your opponent has any skill deficiencies, they should be exploited. For example, if your opponent can't bank or kick very well, this should be factored into your safeties and push-out shots.

Score -- If the score indicates you are winning, you should keep on doing what you have been doing. If you are falling behind you may want to change some aspect of your strategy. For example, if you're falling behind you may want to adjust your offense - defense ratio. If you get way behind in a match you may want to take more "go for broke" type of chances. This strategy philosophy is like a football team that is behind and running out of time—they go for the first down on the fourth down.

113

Judgment -- If you are consistently making errors in judgment, you should revert back to a simpler strategy. For example, if the cue ball is not going exactly where you expect it to go, don't take shots that require finesse shape, rather, accept a little less shape and expect to shoot more safeties than usual.

◆ ◆ ◆

SHOT OR SHAPE

Every time you shoot an offensive shot your goal is to pocket the object ball and get shape for the next ball. These two objectives are not always mutually compatible. If you wanted the best chance of making an object ball you would shoot it at a moderate speed without any english. But, if you want to get shape on the next ball you may have to shoot harder or softer and/or with various types of english. Having to do these things to get shape actually decreases your chance of making the object ball. Therefore, each shot represents a tradeoff in emphasis. You must decide on how much of a chance you are willing to take on missing the object ball for the sake of getting position for the next ball.

Except for safeties, and some two-way shots, pocketing the object ball should always take precedence over getting shape. Knowing this, and shooting as if you know this, are two different things. There will be many times in everyone's pool career when these priorities will get mixed up. The realistic

114

objective should be to reduce these occurrences as much as possible.

The relative importance of shot and shape varies somewhat depending on the skill level of the player. The neophyte assigns 100 percent importance to pocketing the object ball and zero importance to getting shape. As the player's skill progresses, more and more importance is placed on getting shape. By the time the player is at the pro level, getting shape is almost as important as making the object ball. It is not uncommon for good players to occasionally cross over the line allowing shape to become more important than pocketing the object ball; try to keep these occurrences to a minimum.

There are some shots in which only one of the objectives can be realized. For example, if you shoot the object ball into the pocket, you probably won't get good shape. In other instances, if you shoot for shape you will probably miss the object ball. In cases like these you must fight off the tendency to "compromise" by shooting in between and getting neither.

When getting ready to execute a shot, the focus of the brain goes back and forth from pocketing the object ball to getting shape. The brain usually gives precedence to the last thing it thinks about. Therefore, if you want making the object ball to take precedence, think of it immediately before executing the shot (this would be a good argument for a slight pause before the final forward stroke).

Good strategy always calls for sacrificing shape for pocketing the object ball. This does not mean that you have to give up shape entirely, just some degree

115

of shape. Using this philosophy, some shots will be a little more difficult but at least you, rather than your opponent, will be shooting. If, in the process, a shot becomes too difficult, shoot a defensive shot rather than offensive shot.

◆ ◆ ◆

OFFENSE VERSUS DEFENSE

For most players, regardless of skill level, NINE-BALL is largely an offensive game. The beginner probably doesn't know enough about defense to use it effectively and the experienced player doesn't want to shoot a defensive shot because it would mean giving up the table. Both the neophyte and experienced players could probably improve their winning percentages by incorporating more defense into their game strategy.

When defense fails it is probably because it hasn't been used or practiced enough. It is neither fun nor immediately rewarding to practice defense. When an offensive shot is practiced the outcome or value of the shot is immediately obvious, the ball is either pocketed (good) or is missed (bad). The feedback is immediate and decisive which results in an efficient learning process. The result of shooting a safety is subjective, it is neither good nor bad, black nor white, it is usually somewhere in between. Because the result is subjective the learning process is not as efficient. Practicing defensive strategies is like investing in a retirement plan, the rewards are long term but extremely important.

The question of whether to incorporate more or less defense into your strategy can be resolved by carefully observing the result of your defensive action. Try using a little more defense and see if your winning percentage increases. Keep track of who comes out ahead when you initiate a safety. The effectiveness of shooting a safety is usually very subtle. Therefore, the safety should not be evaluated until you or your opponent have taken a few additional shots after the safety.

◆ ◆ ◆

THREE-BALL SEQUENCE

It is often asked, how far ahead should a player look and plan shots? The answer varies depending on the player's competence. A neophyte must be concerned only with the ball that's being shot; the average barroom player plans a two-ball sequence; and the expert plans a three-ball sequence. I know— some players claim to look nine balls in advance— they may have a general idea of how they wish to play each ball but they don't have a specific plan. Suffice to say; if you plan three shots in advance you can successfully compete with anyone, that is, providing you have the other necessary skills.

Some may argue that all players, regardless of skill level, should plan a three-ball sequence. It depends on the individual's goals, objectives, and motivation. If

117

they are participating just for the fun and camaraderie, a one or two ball sequence is adequate. If they are highly competitive and anxious to advance they should progress to a three-ball strategy as soon as possible. Regardless of skill level, when just practicing, all players should aspire to plan a three-ball sequence.

For the player that aspires to progress beyond average a three-ball sequence is not just nice—it is mandatory. The three-ball sequence allows you to make the object ball and get shape on the second ball so that you can get shape on the third ball. For many players it is easier to envision the sequence by looking backwards from the third ball to the present ball. To do this:

1. Pick out a spot on the table where you want the cue ball to be when shooting the third ball (third ball position spot).
2. Then, determine where you would have to be when shooting the second ball (second ball position spot) in order to get position on the third ball.
3. Shoot the first ball so that the cue ball ends up on the second ball position spot.

If it is easier for you to think forward, use this process:

1. Consider where you want the cue ball to be when shooting the second ball?
2. Ask yourself, could you get position on the third ball from there?

3. If not, keep changing position on the second ball until the answer is yes.

Players that plan a two-ball sequence can advance to a three-ball sequence very easily. All that is required is to place the finger at the spot where they want the cue ball for the second ball. This position will automatically take into consideration getting shape on the third ball.

After shooting the first ball, in the three-ball sequence, the next higher numbered ball must be added to the sequence. When adding the new ball the original plan may have to be scrapped and an entirely new plan devised. Don't feel bad about scrapping an old plan and devising a new one. There are many things that may not go as planned on every shot, you must allow for these variables and be flexible.

Planning for a straight-in stop shot on the first ball in a three-ball sequence is usually fine. However, incorporating stop shots for the second and third shot, in a three-ball sequence, may not be such a good idea. Getting perfectly straight-in doesn't always happen. Having an unplanned cut angle is usually trouble, and especially so if you get on the wrong side. Therefore, be cautious about including too many straight-in shots in your three-ball sequence.

Planning a three-ball sequence is obviously important in becoming a good NINE-BALL player. Many players know and believe this but they still don't actually do it. This problem may have a psychological origin. The player doesn't want to commit to a position spot for the third ball because they may be embarrassed if the cue ball doesn't end up there. No one wants to be confronted with his or her errors so blatantly. Without actually picking out the position spot they can fudge a bit and justify why they got where they did. Everyone must decide for himself or herself how much humility they are willing to suffer in order to play a better game of NINE-BALL.

Even the best players must continually monitor their implementation of the three-ball sequence strategy; you should too. Test yourself occasionally—stop, look away from the table and describe your three-ball sequence. Try pointing to the position spot for the third ball. If you fail the test you know that your game has not yet reached its pinnacle. You have simply found a component of your game that can be improved very easily.

◆ ◆ ◆

CHOOSING A POCKET

In your initial table assessment you should look for the best available pocket for each ball. This takes a little thought because some pockets aren't immediately available but will automatically become available as the game progresses. For example, if the 5-ball is blocking the best pocket for the 8-ball, it is not a problem. The pocket should be considered available because the 5-ball will be gone before the 8-ball must be shot.

A ball in the center of the table is easy to get shape on (because there are six pockets to choose from) but it is still more difficult to make (it is the farthest it can be from any pocket) than is generally perceived. Shooting the ball into one of the side pockets offers a big target (12 degrees direction tolerance) but the corner pockets are much more difficult because of the greater distance (5 degrees direction tolerance). Therefore, getting shape for one of the corner pockets is not usually the best option.

As a general rule, the pocket closest to the object ball is the best pocket. This is especially true when comparing corner pockets but not always true when a side pocket is involved. When shooting directly into a side pocket (90 degree approach angle) the side pockets are easier than the corner pockets because they have a larger opening. The opening of a side pocket is generally about a half inch larger than that of a corner pocket. However, as the approach angle becomes smaller, the effective size of the side pocket becomes smaller. At an approach angle of about 70 degrees the effective size of the side pocket is about equal to the corner pocket. At an approach angle of about 20 degrees the effective size becomes zero. The effective pocket size, of the corner pockets, remains about the same regardless of the approach angle.

The effective size of the target area is only one of several options that must be considered when choosing a pocket. The ease of getting the cue ball into position for the shot is probably the next biggest consideration. If you can't get into position to shoot at the easiest pocket you must consider the next easiest pocket.

Having to select a pocket other than the easiest pocket presents somewhat of a problem. Throughout

121

our pool career we condition ourselves to go for shape that allows us to shoot at the closest pocket. Sometimes it is extremely difficult to get shape on an easy pocket but our conditioning makes us go for the shape anyway. We frequently don't get the difficult shape and end up missing the succeeding shot. The moral of this story is that sometimes it is better to go for easy shape into a difficult pocket rather than difficult shape into an easy pocket.

◆ ◆ ◆

CLUSTERS

Clusters are usually a bigger problem in EIGHT-BALL than in NINE-BALL. This is because fifteen object balls are used in the game of EIGHT-BALL (greater density of balls) and only nine object balls are used in NINE-BALL. Also, NINE-BALL is generally played on a bigger table, which further reduces the density of balls.

Before shooting your first shot you should determine if there are any clustered balls that require special attention. If there are clusters, you should immediately formulate a plan to deal with them either sooner or later. The timing as to when the cluster should be broken up is largely a function of the player's skill. Highly skilled players should attempt to break up the cluster as early in the game as possible. If an early attempt fails another attempt can be tried at a later time. However, if the player is not capable of a sustained run, the attempted break up should be postponed for as long as possible (the cluster may become your opponent's problem).

Cue-ball nudge -- The preferred way of dealing with a cluster is to have the cue ball run into it after pocketing an object ball. The opportunity for using the cue-ball nudge technique depends on two aspects: where the object ball is in relation to the cluster and where the next object ball is (can you break up the cluster and still get shape). Generally, the closer the first object ball is to the cluster the easier it is to make the cue-ball strike the cluster accurately. Not only do you want to hit the cluster, you want to do it in a controlled manner so you know where each of the clustered balls will go and where the cue ball will end up.

The proper speed of this type of break out shot is critical. If you are sure the cue ball will run into the cluster you can shoot it hard enough to move the clustered balls where desired and still keep the cue ball under control. But, if you accidentally miss the cluster, the cue ball will roll much farther than anticipated. Keep in mind, it is usually to your opponent's advantage if you break up a cluster and don't get shape on the next ball.

Because of the uncertainty of where the cue ball may end up, it is desirable to have the next object ball near a pocket where it can be made easily. The closer the next object ball is to a pocket the greater the chance you can take on breaking up the cluster. For example if the 5-ball is in the jaws of a corner pocket the shooter can try to break up a cluster, while shooting the 4-ball, regardless of where it is in relation to the cluster.

Shooting directly at clusters -- In some circumstances the object ball may be a part of the cluster. This means you must shoot directly at the cluster with the objective being either to pocket a ball or execute a safety. This cluster busting technique has an advantage in that you have control of all the balls involved including the cue ball. Before shooting at the cluster it must be examined closely. Having the balls close together makes it easy to determine what direction each ball will go when struck from a particular direction.

Figures 6-1 shows several different strategies that can be used when dealing with clusters.

Combinations: In **Figure 6-1A** the 1-ball can be shot into the 6-ball; it will carom off the 6-ball and go into the corner pocket. If the 7-ball is the object ball, it can be shot slightly to the left of center; it will carom off the 8-ball, into the 9-ball and then go into the corner pocket.

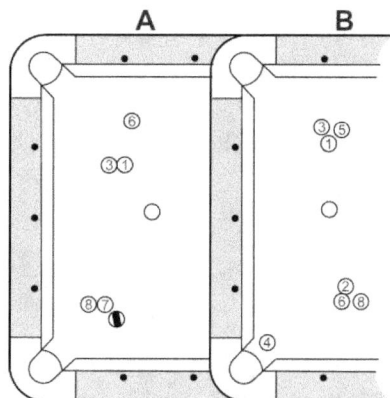

FIGURE 6-1. (A) The 1-ball or the 7-ball can be made with a combination. (B) By hitting the 1-ball the 3-ball can be banked into the 4-ball. A carom shot off the 2-ball can pocket the 4-ball.

Banks: Occasionally the balls in the cluster are set up for a bank shot. **Figure 6-1B** shows some possible bank shots. The 1-ball can be shot head-on; the 3-ball will bank into the 4-ball putting it into the corner pocket. At the same time, the 5-ball may bank off the side rail and go into the opposite side pocket.

If the 2-ball is the object ball it can be shot into the 6-ball making it cross-corner. Another option would be to barely hit the 2-ball on the right side and caroming the cue ball into the 4-ball. With this type of carom shot, the tendency is to hit the 2-ball too full causing the cue ball to hit the end cushion. For that reason it is advisable to put left english on the cue ball so that if it strikes the end rail first it will still have a chance of rebounding into and making the 4-ball.

125

Safeties: The 3-ball in **Figure 6-2C** can be nudged on the right side leaving the cue ball behind the 5-ball. The 4-ball can be struck head on using a stun stroke. The cue ball will remain behind the 6- and 9-ball.

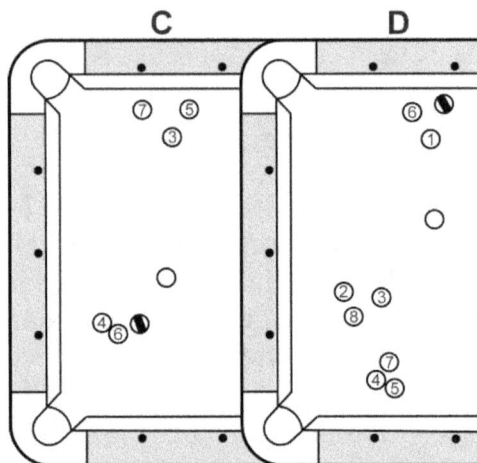

FIGURE 6-2. (C) The cue ball can be hidden behind the 5-ball. The 4-ball can be struck head on with a stop shot. (D) Possible 1- 9-ball combination. The 2-ball can be used to break up a cluster.

Blast away: In some situations it is advisable to give the balls a good ride and hope for the best. The lower your skill level the more viable this strategy is. Also, the more balls that can be moved, the more viable this technique is. When using this technique, try to strike the object ball head on so the cue ball doesn't run around the table and possibly scratch.

The 1-ball in **Figure 6-2D** can be shot head-on at high speed using a stun stroke. The 9-ball has a good chance of going into one of the side pockets. The 6-ball will bank into the clustered balls on the other side of the table and possibly make one of them.

If the 2-ball is the object ball the same blast technique can be used. That is, shoot head-on into the 2-ball as hard as possible. The 2-ball will rebound off the end cushion into the three clustered balls. Depending on how the cluster is struck, the 5-ball may bank into the opposite corner pocket and/or the 7-ball could go into the upper side pocket. If you don't think any ball will go in, you could stop the cue ball (for a safety) behind the 3-and 8-ball. If you think a ball will be made you could follow the 2-ball to the cushion hoping for another shot at the 2-ball.

The efficacy of blasting away at a cluster of balls depends on several things. One factor is whether or not the object ball can be hit head-on. If you can hit the object ball head-on you can stop the cue ball. Stopping the cue ball reduces its chance of scratching or having the cue ball go somewhere you don't want it to go. The second factor is the number of balls you can move. The more balls you move the better chance you have of slopping one in (like on the break shot). The third, and probably the most important factor is the skill level of the players. The higher your skill level the less chance you should take on a blast shot.

If there is a chance of slopping the 9-ball in, the blast shot must be given a higher priority. A general rule for blasting at the 9-ball requires that you take into consideration the chance of beating your opponent. **If the chance of beating your opponent is smaller than the chance of slopping in the 9-ball then—go for it**. For example if you beat your opponent only 40 percent of the time and there is a 50 percent chance of slopping in the 9-ball, then go for the blast shot. Conversely, if you beat your opponent 60 percent of the time and there is a 50 percent chance of slopping in the 9-ball then <u>don't</u> go for the shot.

Note: There are a number of other factors that affect the odds for and against going for a blast shot. Of these the most important are: the number of balls on the table, the possibility of getting shape after the blast shot, the possibility of leaving your opponent something good, and the probabilities of all the alternative shots. If you have a computer handy you should factor in these other variables, if not, go for the rule of thumb.

◆ ◆ ◆

BALLS ON CUSHION

Balls that are on a cushion may present a problem. One of the problems is that they don't bank well because there is a high potential for a double kiss. Aside from a bank shot, there are only two potential pockets (at each end of the cushion) in which they can be made. Reducing the potential pockets from six to two presents a problem. On some tables an object ball won't go down the side rail past the side pocket without being deflected off course. This further limits the potential pockets to only one.

The best way to shoot a rail shot depends on how far the object ball is from the pocket and the cut angle. The book *THE SCIENCE OF POCKET BILLIARDS* has an entire chapter on the best way to shoot rail shots. As a general rule, for moderate cut-angle shots, the cue ball should be aimed to strike the rail slightly before striking the object ball with a little cushion side english.

Another difficult situation results when two consecutive balls are on the same cushion. For example, when the 4- and 5-ball are on the same side rail near the side pocket. This situation presents two problems. First, it is difficult to get a shallow cut angle at the 4-ball because the 5-ball is in the way. And second, even if you can make the 4-ball it is difficult to get back to the same rail for good shape on the 5-ball. The solution is to move one of the balls off the cushion before they have to be shot.

When evaluating the probability of running a ball down the rail you must take into account the size and shape of the corner pockets. On some tables it is extremely difficult to run a ball down the rail into a corner pocket. The more difficult the pocket is for rail shots, the smaller the cut angle must be to insure making the object ball. As the problems involved with shooting a rail shot increase, the bank options start to look increasingly better.

◆ ◆ ◆

SHAPE OPTIONS

How to get shape on each ball probably constitutes a player's biggest strategy decision. The following is a discussion of some of the most common techniques for getting shape.

Random shape -- When people first start playing pool they usually depend on random shape for all their shape. This is reasonable because when you are first learning to play there are other things (like hitting the cue ball) that occupy your mind. As your competence increases you realize that relying on random shape won't get you to the next level of play. Therefore, most players naturally rely less and less on random shape as their pocketing skills increase. However, there are some vestiges of random shape tendencies that linger; they sometimes reoccur when we are shooting either very difficult shots or very easy shots.

There are times when the intermediate player tries to get shape but not for a specific pocket. For example, assume the 9-ball is on the center spot and the 8-ball is nearly straight-in about one diamond from a corner pocket. The intermediate player may try to leave the cue ball close to the 9-ball and trust to chance that it will leave an easy shot at one of the six pockets. This random technique works fairly well until the player's skill increases. The problem is that as the player gets progressively better at controlling the cue ball, the cue ball will stop closer and closer to the 9-ball. In this case ability increased but strategy

stagnated. Stopping the cue ball too close to the
object ball severely limits the chance of a shot into
any of the pockets. At some point in the learning
process, the player must stop trying to position the
cue ball close to the 9-ball and start shooting for
shape at a specific pocket.

How much shape -- Before executing a shot, you
should ask yourself; "How close do I want to get to
the next object ball?" and "How much of a cut angle
will I accept?"

It's nice to get close to the object ball but trying to
get too close may cause problems." If the shot is
straight in, getting within a few inches of the object
ball does not present a problem. But, if it must be cut
into a pocket it may present a problem. For example,
assume a ball must be cut 30 degrees into a pocket; it
won't be a problem at a distance of one foot but if the
cue ball is only an inch from the object ball, the shot
is much harder to judge.

When deciding on the optimum cut angle, nearly
every shot represents a conflict of interest. You have
to make a choice between having a straight-in shot
(easy shot but difficult getting shape) and having a
cut angle (more difficult shot but easier to get shape).
All players must find the balance that works best for
themselves. This can only be done by careful
observation and analysis.

Slow or "back and forth" --**Figure 6-3** shows a
typical shot. If the 8-ball is shot very slowly the cue
ball will stop for a shot at the 9-ball. However, what
usually happens is that the cue ball usually rolls too

far and the shooter is left in a difficult cut on the 9-ball. The alternative is to shoot hard enough so the cue-ball rebounds to the opposite side rail then back to where the 8-ball was. The cue ball has to travel much farther but the shot is much less speed sensitive. When in doubt, always go back and forth rather than shoot an extremely soft shot. This philosophy holds true even when the cue ball has to go back and forth the long way.

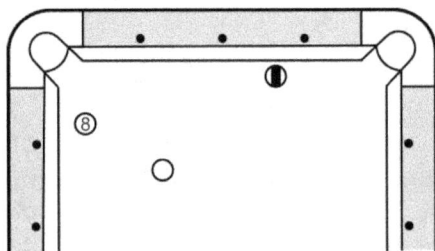

FIGURE 6-3. Shooting the 8-ball and getting shape on the 9-ball is a speed sensitive shot.

Right side–wrong side -- Getting on the "wrong side" of an object ball means the cue ball will be going in the wrong direction for shape on the next ball. **Figure 6-4** shows a typical situation. From cue ball position "A" (right side) the 2-ball can be shot into the side pocket while getting easy shape on the 3-ball. However, a small error in cue-ball position, as shown by cue ball position "B", will make it extremely difficult to get shape on the 3-ball.

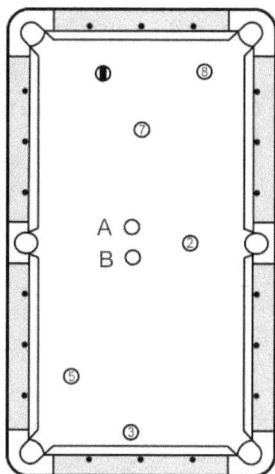

FIGURE 6-4. Shape on the 3-ball is easy from cue ball position "A" but difficult from "B".

Avoiding scratches -- When the cue ball has to strike a cushion, there is always a chance that it might go into a pocket. When we first start learning to play pool we have to be concerned about scratching as the cue ball comes off the object ball. As our skill progresses we must make the cue ball travel farther for position, and consequently more cushions are struck in the process. The more cushions struck, the greater the chance of scratching.

The route the cue ball has to take must always be evaluated with regard to potential scratches. If there is a good chance that the cue ball will scratch, choose a different route even if it means accepting less shape.

Side or end rail – Assume a situation where the object ball is at one end of the table and the next ball is at the other end (as shown in **Figure 6-5**). The

133

question is, do you want to position the cue ball to go
either to the end or side rail for shape on the next
ball. Should the cue ball be in position **"B"** or **"F"**?
From position **"B"** the 8-ball can be made and the
cue ball will go to cushion **"C"** and then back to the
other end of the table for the shot at the 9-ball. From
position **"F"** the 8-ball can be made and the cue ball
will go to cushions **"Y,"** then **"U,"** then back to the
other end of the table for a shot at the 9-ball.

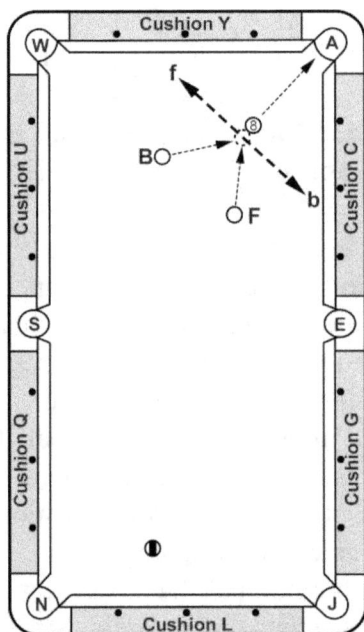

**FIGURE 6-5. You must decide if it is better to
go to the side or end rail for best shape on
the next ball.**

In the example shown in **Figure 6-5** it probably doesn't matter much—position can be gotten on the 9-ball just as easily either way. But, if the 9-ball and/or the 8-ball were moved a little, either the side or the end rail may be best. So how do you determine which rail is best?

To determine the best position, draw a line from the 8-ball (first object ball) to the pocket. Draw another line through the ghost ball perpendicular to the first line (line **"b f"** in **Figure 6-5**). Now you have to make a judgment—would you rather have the cue ball going in direction **"b"** or in direction **"f"** for shape on the next ball? Your answer will dictate whether you should use the side or end rail for best shape on the next ball.

Can you reach it -- There are areas on the table where it is hard to reach the cue ball. Stretching for a shot reduces accuracy so these areas should be avoided as much as possible. A mechanical bridge can be used but when it is used the ability to judge english, speed, and aim generally drops considerably. It is usually better to accept a little longer shot than to have to reach for a shot.

Figure 6-6 shows the areas on the table where, if shooting in the direction of the arrows, the cue ball is difficult to reach. The best way to avoid these difficult shots is to visualize shooting the next shot with the cue ball at the expected position spot. Many good players simulate what they expect to be their next shot, by actually getting into shooting position. If, for any reason, they are not comfortable with their shooting position, they choose another position for the cue ball.

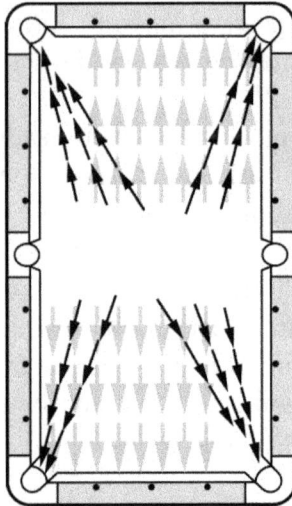

FIGURE 6-6. Arrows indicate the area and shooting direction where the cue ball is difficult to reach.

◆ ◆ ◆

9-BALL COMBINATIONS

In the game of EIGHT-BALL you must constantly be aware of where the 8-ball is so you don't accidentally knock it into a pocket. In the game of NINE-BALL it is just the opposite; you must be aware of where the 9-ball is so that you can make it out of sequence.

Ride the 9-ball -- Sometimes it is good policy to give the 9-ball a good ride (hit it as hard as is practical and hope it finds a pocket). This is especially true if you know you can keep the cue ball under control and leave it in a safe place. Giving the 9-ball a ride is a great equalizer, a 50 percent shooter can ride the 9-ball almost as well as an 80 percent shooter.

When giving the 9-ball a ride there are usually other balls that are moved as well and are likely to go into a pocket. If you have a choice, always try to make the moving ball strike the stationary ball at a half-ball hit. This insures that each ball involved in the collision will speed away after the collision.

Skill level and odds -- When watching NINE-BALL players, of different skill levels, you may notice that the players with less skill attempt more 9-ball combinations. Mathematical analysis of the probabilities confirms the validity of this strategy.

Players must consider several factors when contemplating a 9-ball combination. They must consider the probability of making the combination as opposed to the probability of running the remaining balls. The probability of shooting again even if the 9-ball is missed must also be considered.

The probability of making the 9-ball combination must be estimated by considering the ball layout and the player's skill. For example, if the player can make the combination one in five attempts the probability for making the shot is 20 percent. The chance of running the table depends on the player's shot making ability and the number of balls still on the table. It must be kept in mind that missing the combination does not automatically mean you lose the game. There is a chance that the opponent will not run the table and you will have another chance to win the game.

Recognize opportunities -- When the 9-ball is near a pocket you should always look for an opportunity for a combination shot. The closer the 9-ball is to a pocket, the greater the chance of making it with a combination. However, just because the 9-ball is not near a pocket does not mean that it can't be made in a combination. The closer the 9-ball is to the object ball the easier it is to determine if there is a chance of a combination. For example, if the 5- and 9-ball are in contact with each other, it is easy to determine the direction the 9-ball will go when the 5-ball is struck. Also check for carom opportunities, in some situations the 9-ball can be caromed off another ball then go into a pocket. Keep in mind that the two balls do not have to be in contact to present combination or carom possibilities. The same opportunities exist when the balls are separated but the aim tolerance becomes smaller.

Many viable 9-ball shots are passed up simply because they are overlooked. After each break shot, challenge yourself to find the easiest 9-ball combination or carom shot. The easiest shot may not be a viable shot but by identifying the easiest shot you won't overlook any opportunities.

◆ ◆ ◆

SHOOTING THE 9-BALL

There is a tendency for many players to choke while shooting the 9-ball. This is because it is the "money ball" and has more emotion associated with it than any of the other balls. Another unique thing about shooting at the 9-ball is that you don't have to get shape on a succeeding ball. In order to make the 9-ball more like any other ball, pick out a spot on the table where you want the cue ball to end up. Keeping your mind occupied with the cue-ball's position will relieve some of the anxiety of shooting the 9-ball.

◆ ◆ ◆

EXAMPLES AND ANALYSIS

In the following examples some solutions to the problems are explored. The reader is encouraged to try to think of alternate solutions as well.

ANALYSIS OF FIGURE 6-7:
    Problem: The problem with this table configuration is the two clusters consisting of the 4- and 6-ball and the 7- and 8-ball.
    Commentary: The 4-6 cluster can easily be broken up while shooting the 1-ball. The 7-8 cluster is a much bigger problem because there are no other balls in the vicinity that can be shot while breaking them up. The best chance for a run is to shoot hard when breaking up the 4-6 cluster hoping that one of the

balls will go to the other end of the table so that it can be used to break up the 7-9 cluster. If that doesn't work, try to get shape on the 3-9 combination while shooting the 2-ball. Another solution is to go directly from the 1-ball to the 2-ball to the 3-9 combination without breaking up the either cluster. That way, even if you miss the 9-ball combination your opponent will still have two difficult clusters to deal with.

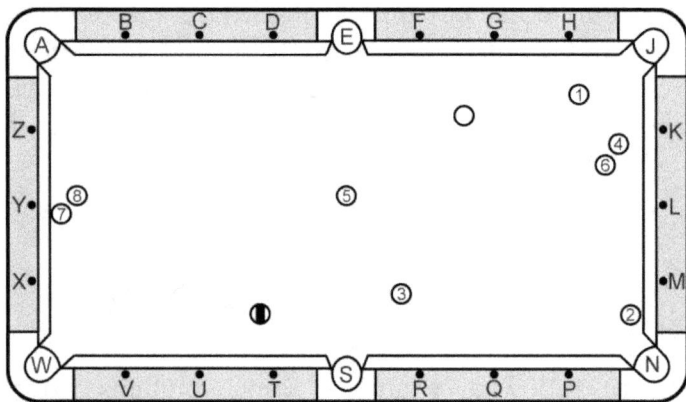

FIGURE 6-7. Example problems and solutions.

If you get stuck having to shoot at the 7-ball don't despair, there is a reasonably good safety possibility. Try to get the cue ball somewhere in the vicinity of the 5-ball. Shoot the 7-ball into the end rail toward diamond "**Y**." The 7-ball will rebound into the 8-ball and stop; the cue ball will go two rails to the other end of the table.

ANALYSIS OF FIGURE 6-8:
Problem: The balls are spread apart in what looks to be an easy table. However, even a top professional

would have trouble running this table because the cue ball must travel back and forth the length of the table several times in order to get shape.

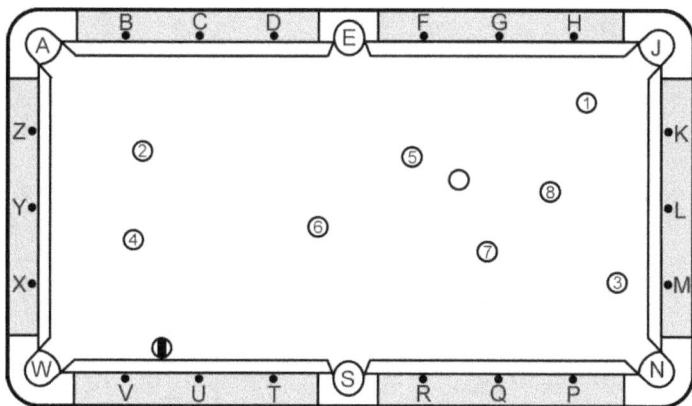

FIGURE 6-8. Example problems and solutions.

Commentary: There are no easy solutions here. The best thing to do is to try to run the balls. If you don't get good shape on a ball, shoot a safety.

ANALYSIS OF FIGURE 6-9:

Problem: The problem with this table configuration is that consecutive balls are positioned on the same rail. It would be difficult to shoot the 3-ball and get back to that rail for a good shot at the 4-ball. The same problem exists for the 7- and 8-ball.

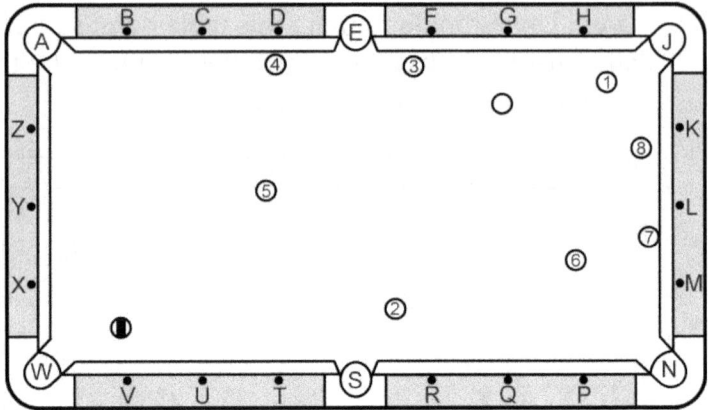

FIGURE 6-9. Example problems and solutions.

Commentary: The 1- and 2-ball can be pocketed fairly easy. In making the 2-ball the cue ball should be positioned for a bank shot at the 3-ball into pocket **"S."** That should solve the 2-3 problem. When pocketing the 7-ball, less than perfect shape can be accepted on the 8-ball because getting shape on the 9-ball should be easy (no english is required in shooting the 8-ball therefore, it can be hit more accurately).

ANALYSIS OF FIGURE 6-10:

Problem: This table has a variety of problems. The cue ball has to be moved the length of the table in going from the 1-ball to the 2-ball. The 4- and 8-ball are clustered and the 5- and 7-ball are on the side rail near the side pocket. And there is yet another problem; the 3-ball is in the most difficult position possible (by the rail adjacent to the side pocket).

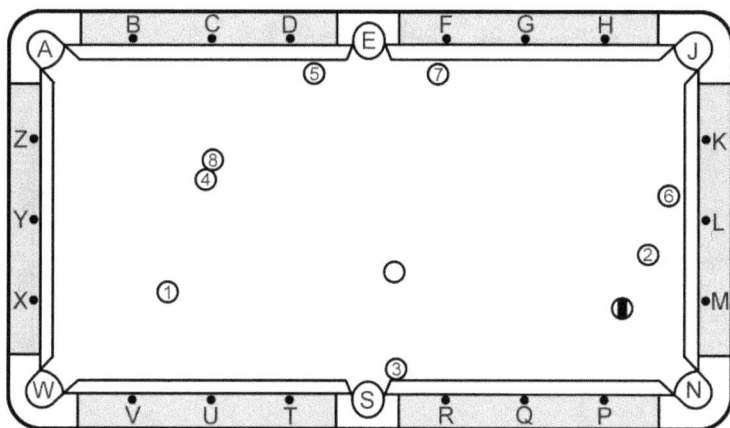

FIGURE 6-10. Example problems and solutions.

Commentary: The 4-8 cluster can be nudged with the cue ball after making the 1-ball. The fact that the 5- and 7-ball are not consecutive balls makes them a little easier but still difficult. The tighter the corner pockets, the more difficult they are to run down the rail. If the corner pockets are real tight consideration should be given to banking one or both of them into side pocket **"S."** The 3-ball is a serious problem. It would be difficult to make it into pocket **"N,"** or even bank it into pocket **"J"** (because the cue ball will scratch in pocket **"S"**). Shooting it into pocket **"W"** is difficult because it would have to pass the jaws of pocket **"S."**

Because of all the problems it might be best to shoot the 1-ball and get position for a carom shot off the 2-ball into the 9-ball. If that doesn't work, shoot a safety when shooting the 2-ball.

ANALYSIS OF FIGURE 6-11:

143

Problem: The 1-ball can't be hit.

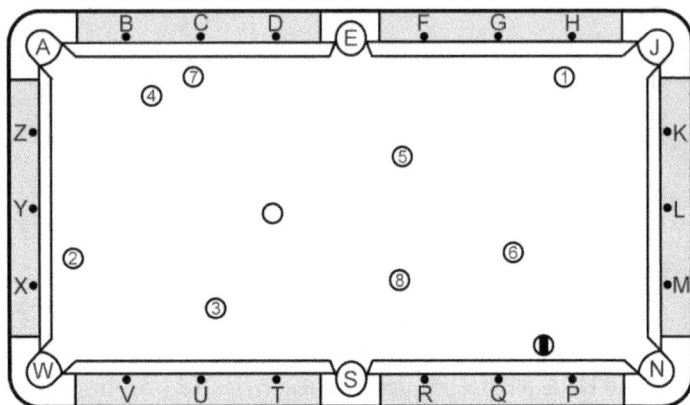

FIGURE 6-11. Example problems and solutions.

Commentary: A jump shot can be used to hit the 1-ball but there are several better options. The 1-ball can be hit by kicking at the end rail between diamonds **"J"** and **"K."** But just hitting the object ball wouldn't accomplish much. There is a chance the 1-ball can be pocketed by kicking either to the end rail between diamonds **"Y"** and **"Z"** or kicking at the side rail near diamond **"G"** using a curve shot. However, even if the 1-ball was pocketed, neither of these options would allow for a good shot at the 2-ball. Another option would be to push-out.

In deciding where to push to, you must take into consideration your opponent's physical stature and skills. If your opponent can't bank as well as you, push to position **"H-L"** for a bank shot into pocket **"N."** If your opponent can't draw as well as you, leave a long straight-in shot. Your opponent may make the 1-ball but won't get shape on the 2-ball.

144

ANALYSIS OF FIGURE 6-12:

Problem: How to make the 1-ball.

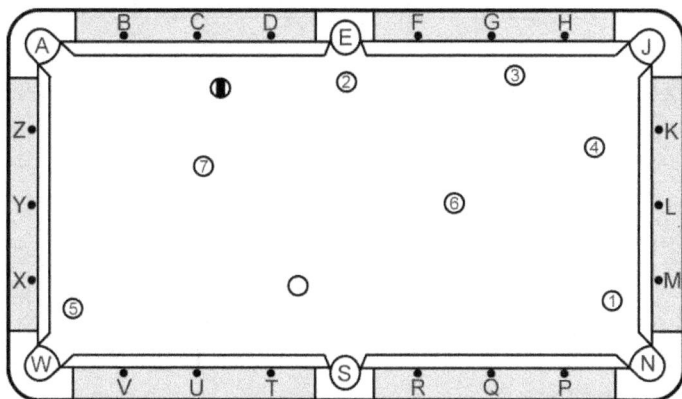

FIGURE 6-12. Example problems and solutions.

Commentary: The 1-ball can be cut into pocket
"N." The problem with this shot is that the 1-ball has
to be cut so thin that there is a danger of missing it all
together. To help insure against a foul, a little right
english should be used. This way, if the shot is cut
too thin, the cue ball will rebound off the rail and into
the object ball thus avoiding a foul.

The 1-ball can also be banked into pocket **"W."**
To avoid a double kiss, the 1-ball will have to be cut
a few extra degrees (to the right) and right english put
on the cue ball (to decrease the cut angle). The target
pocket will play bigger than it is because the 5-ball is
acting as a funnel.

ANALYSIS OF FIGURE 6-13:

Problem: Two clusters prevent an easy run.

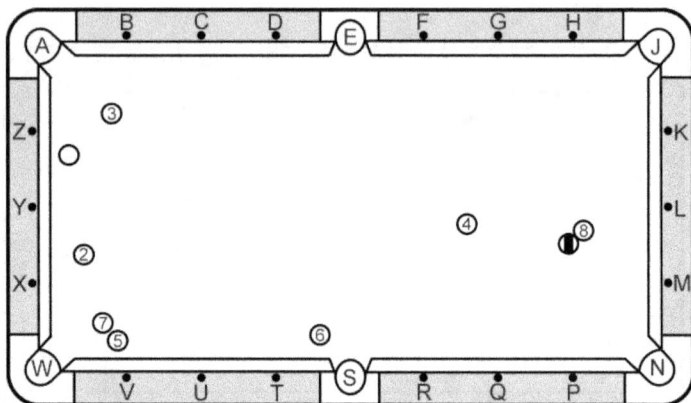

FIGURE 6-13. Example problems and solutions.

Commentary: The 5-7 cluster can be broken up by making the 2-ball carom off the 7-ball as it goes into the corner pocket. But there is a better way of handling this situation. Shoot the 2-ball cleanly into the pocket and leave the 5-7 cluster undisturbed. Shoot the 3-ball and get shape such that the 4-ball can be shot directly into the 9-ball. If everything goes well the 9-ball will carom off the 8-ball and go into pocket **"N."** If the 9-ball is missed, your opponent will have to contend with the 5-7 cluster.

ANALYSIS OF FIGURE 6-14:

Problem: The 5- and 7-ball are clustered preventing an easy run.

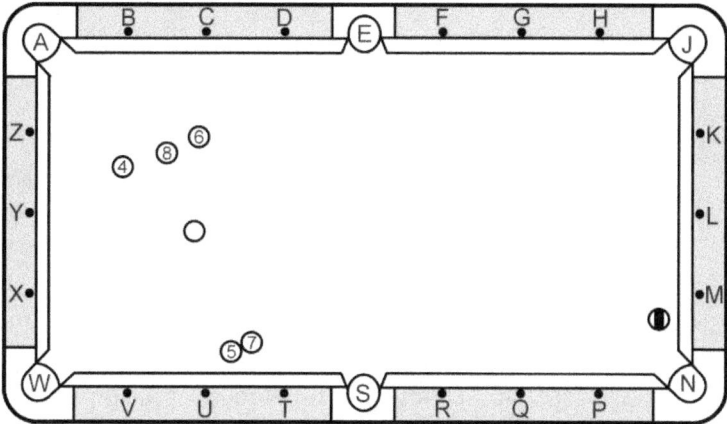

FIGURE 6-14. Example problems and solutions.

Commentary: It may be possible to draw the cue ball back into the cluster while shooting the 4-ball. But the danger with this shot is that the cue ball may freeze up to the 5-ball preventing a shot. The 5-and 7-ball are aligned directly toward pocket **"J."** The 4-ball can be pocketed and the cue-ball stopped for a kick shot to side rail at the 5-ball. The 7-ball will go into pocket **"J."**

However, there is a better solution. The 4-ball can be hit a little to the right of center with a little top english. The 4-ball will go two rails and end up near the 9-ball. The cue ball will hide behind the 6- and 8-ball for a safety. If your opponent fouls you may get to shoot an easy 4-9 combination. If something goes wrong, you still have the 5-7 cluster to prevent your opponent from running out.

◆ ◆ ◆

STRATEGY OVERVIEW

It is difficult to be specific in suggesting proper NINE-BALL strategy because of the many situations requiring different strategies. As in the game of chess, a general strategy can be suggested, but the number of pieces and positions are so numerous that one specific strategy cannot be used exclusively.

Appropriate strategy is dictated, to a large extent, by the individual's ability. For example, a beginner need not be concerned about the position of the 4-ball while shooting the 1-ball. As ability improves the player must look and plan further in advance. Be careful not to let your knowledge of strategy lag behind your ability; once you're _able_ to run the table, your strategy must _allow_ you to run the table. It is one thing to know strategy and quite another thing to employ it. Experiment with various strategy options during practice play. Even beginners should try to learn the finer points of strategy so that when their ability allows, they will be properly prepared. Being aware of the various strategy options will encourage beginners to stretch their abilities.

The strategy of professional players should be observed and studied at every opportunity. Attend as many professional tournaments as possible. Purchase and study all the NINE-BALL videotapes your

148

finances will allow. When viewing a tape try to anticipate the player's strategy. If the professional does something that you don't expect, try to determine why.

When playing a friendly practice game, discuss strategy with your opponent while the game is in progress. Discuss all the strategy options that you can both collectively think of. This will help you recognize more options when playing a serious game.

Each time you miss a ball or lose a game, try to isolate and identify the cause. The problem may be the lack of ability but quite often it can be traced to an error in strategy. The strategy error usually occurs one, two, or more shots before the miss occurs. The sooner strategy errors are identified, the sooner they can be corrected.

Try to utilize a variety of strategy techniques while practicing. Usually, strategy mistakes are made because the player is not aware of the options available at all times. Players that are not aware of the strategy options cannot possibly recognize strategy errors. If errors are not recognized they can't be corrected and thus the learning process is stymied. Quite frequently, strategy options are not recognized because of a particular mind-set, the brain stops thinking about strategy when the first option is identified. Try not to be a victim of this mind set.

Another way of learning appropriate strategy is to practice on paper. Analyzing hypothetical situations on paper will allow more time for thinking about strategy options. The extra time generally reveals more options and the best option is more often identified. The paper training conditions the mind to explore all strategy options. This training will transfer to actual play.

Good strategy doesn't elicit raves from the spectators but it does win games. Players that employ superior strategy win consistently and seemingly without effort because they are not forced to make spectacular shots.

◆ ◆ ◆

CHAPTER 7

TOURNAMENTS

T he main competitive format for the game of NINE-BALL is *tournaments*. Anyone that is serious about the game will eventually compete in some type of tournament.

There are several different types of tournaments; each can be conducted in a variety of ways with different charts, rules, etc. Probably no tournament can be completely fair and impartial; weak players may be matched against strong players and some players will have to play more matches than others— but such is life.

Here are some common terms that apply to tournaments.

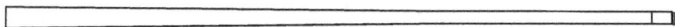

Game: A single contest between two players.

Set: Two or more consecutive games between the same players.

Match: One or more games or sets, between two players, to decide the individual winner.

Race-to-X: A predetermined number (X) of wins, which constitutes a set (or match). For example, a set consisting of a "race-to-5" means whoever wins 5 games first wins the set.

♦♦♦

TYPES OF TOURNAMENTS

There are several different types of tournaments but the three most common are: The *round robin, single elimination,* and *double elimination.* An example of a tournament chart for each of these tournaments is shown in **Figure 7-1**.

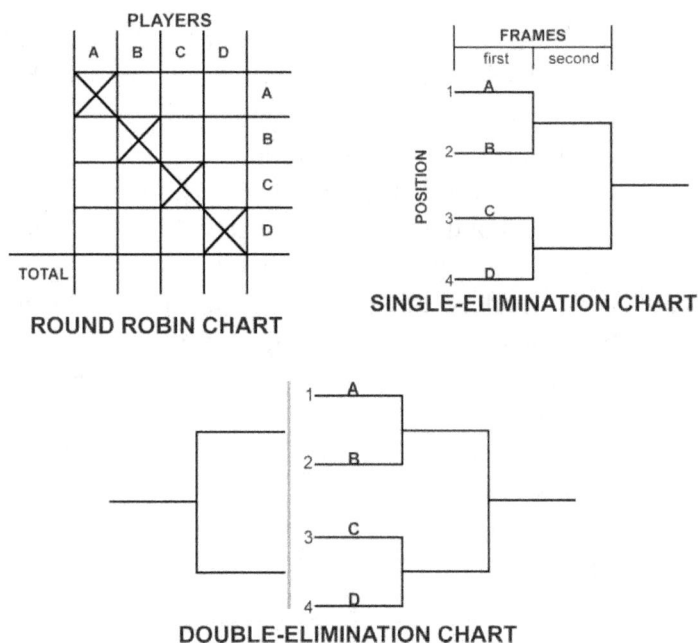

ROUND ROBIN CHART

SINGLE-ELIMINATION CHART

DOUBLE-ELIMINATION CHART

FIGURE 7-1. Examples of three different tournament charts.

A **round robin** tournament is a contest in which each participant is matched against every other participant. The basic concept is to determine the player's ability relative to the entire group rather than the individuals within the group. This type of tournament eliminates the inequities of some players having to play against stronger or weaker players by virtue of a chance drawing. The number of participants is limited only by the time available. The number of matches required, to determine the winner, can be calculated using the formula $(x)(x-1)/2 =$ number of matches (x represents the number of participants). The required number of matches increases faster than the number of participants; for example, with five participants 10 matches are required, with ten participants 45 matches are required.

A **single-elimination** tournament means a player who loses one match is eliminated from the tournament. The winner of each frame advances to the succeeding frame and is matched with another player with an identical record. Play continues until only one player is without a loss; he or she is the tournament winner.

A **double-elimination** tournament means each participant must lose twice before being eliminated from the tournament. The double-elimination tournament is simply an extension of the single-elimination tournament. An additional flow chart is used for the players that suffer one loss. This chart is called the *loser's chart* or *bracket, one loss bracket*, or *second-chance bracket*. Unless otherwise specified, the winner of the second-chance bracket must beat the winner of the winner's bracket <u>twice</u> in order to win the tournament.

153

How the various tournament charts are used, how byes are used, and many other things are discussed in detail in the book *THE SCIENCE OF POCKET BILLIARDS.*

♦♦♦

TOURNAMENT DETAILS

In order for a tournament to be successful it must be promoted. If you plan to participate in, or promote a tournament, here are some of the things that should be addressed prior to the tournament.

1. Location: Even if everybody knows where the tournament is to be played, the location should be spelled out. Being very specific about the location will help new people find the venue. After all, getting new people to attend is one of the prime incentives for having a tournament.
2. Date and time: The date and starting time should be announced as far in advance as possible. It is best to be firm about the starting time, if a player is not there on time, start the tournament anyway.
3. Format: The type of tournament (round robin, double- or single-elimination) should be specified. If it is a race to a specific number of wins it should be so stated. If the tournament is limited to a specific number of players, that fact should be specified.
4. Entry fee: The entry fee often indicates the quality of player that will be attending. A low entry fee

will draw a large number of participants that are not very skilled. A high entry fee will draw fewer participants but they will have a higher skill level.

5. Payout: First place prize money and the number of places that will be paid is usually announced before the tournament. If there is added money (by the promoter) it should be stated. Added money is the amount paid out over and above the total collected for entry fees.

> Note: Be skeptical when you see "guaranteed first place prize of $xxx." In the fine print it may stipulate, "based on a specified minimum number of entries."

6. Phone number: A phone number and mailing address should be given. Be sure that everybody that answers the phone is prepared to answer questions like: directions, lodging, dress code, smoking or non-smoking, etc.

7. Equipment: The size of the tables and possibly the pocket size should be specified. Some players may ask about the type of cloth or brand of table and cue ball being used.

8. Participant restrictions: Is the tournament open to anyone willing to pay the entry fee or is it restricted to players of a specific skill level. If all skill levels are encouraged to attend, is a handicapping system used? If so, what kind?

◆◆◆

RUNNING A TOURNAMENT

Tournament director -- The person that is in charge of running the tournament is called a *tournament director*. The tournament director must assign initial playing positions for each player and determine when and where (what table) each match will take place. The tournament director should know enough about the game of NINE-BALL to be able to referee fouls and arbitrate disagreements.

In the larger tournaments, the tournament director is usually experienced and is able to conduct the tournament with few disruptions. However, in some of the smaller barroom tournaments many of the players will assume they know more than the tournament director and there will be arguments. The best way to resolve these disruptions is by deferring to a written set of house rules. If the house does not have a set of rules, rules set forth by the Billiard Congress of America, or some other recognized organization, should be used.

One of the main functions of a tournament director is to observe close shots to determine whether or not a foul is committed. Most average players are not knowledgeable enough to monitor the close call situations. If tournament directors do not feel they are qualified to recognize fouls, they should assign that task to a more qualified person. The players should agree on the competence of the observer before the shot is executed; this will avoid arguments after the call is made.

In small neighborhood tournaments, everyone should be required to run the tournament occasionally. This will allow everyone to get familiar with the charts and also get a perspective on all the trouble and toil involved. A person (tournament director) that has to resolve all the petty bickering is less likely to bicker as a player.

Tournament date -- When contemplating having a tournament, the most important thing to consider is conflicting tournaments or activities that may be scheduled for the same time and date. Selecting the best date may mean having to coordinate with your competitors.

For barroom tournaments, there is usually a conflict between what the business wants and what the participants want. The bar manager would like to schedule the tournament on nights that are otherwise slow. The participants would like the tournament scheduled for the nights that they will be in the bar anyway. Scheduling a tournament on a slow night may sound like a good business practice but the tournament may fail due to lack of participation. If people don't want to go to a bar on a particular night they probably have a good reason for not going. That same reason may keep them from participating in the pool tournament. The best night for a tournament should be found by trial and error. It may turn out that the best night for a tournament is neither the slowest night nor the busiest night.

Participants -- Start the tournament **on time**; do not wait for the stragglers. If you are having only one

157

tournament, and never expect to have another, it may be prudent to wait for the stragglers. This will insure the maximum number of participants. However, if it is to be a recurring tournament, waiting for the stragglers may be the demise of future tournaments. Waiting for the stragglers will only encourage more, and later, stragglers. This will cause the tournaments to end later and later in the evening. Sooner or later many of the working people will have to drop out and participation will suffer.

Never cancel a tournament just because a specific number of people don't show up. The best way to create a discontented patron is to cancel a tournament after that person has adjusted their schedule to attend the tournament. Discontent is absolutely contradictory to the promoter's purpose of having a tournament.

Rules -- The tournament rules should be posted at the site for all participants to read. A standard set of rules can be used such as the *BILLIARD CONGRESS OF AMERICA* rules. Even when a standard set of rules is used, additional house rules should also be posted. The following are some of the issues the house rules should address.

What precipitates a forfeiture?
Legality of jump, massé, and curve shots.
Who calls fouls?
Who racks?
Are balls off table spotted or not?
What constitutes a "blatant" foul (loss of game)?
It should be stated, in writing, that the tournament director will have the final word in <u>all</u> disputes.

Seeding -- In a *seeded tournament* the player's ranking is taken into consideration in the assignment of opponents in the early frames. It is structured to ensure that those players that have the greatest skill are not matched against each other in the early rounds. The lowest ranked players play among themselves in the early rounds. As the tournament advances, progressively higher ranked players begin to participate.

When a tournament is seeded, the entry fee may be higher for the better players. A seeded, 64-position single elimination tournament, could be structured as follows: The 32 lowest ranked players ($30 entry fee) play in the first frame; the 16 victorious players are matched with players ranked 17 through 32 ($40 entry fee); the 16 victorious players from this group are matched with players ranked 1 through 16 ($50 entry fee); the remaining frames are played in the normal manner.

The seeded format has desirable features for both the low ranked players and the high ranked players. The low ranked players like it because they don't have to play a high ranked player in the early rounds, and their entry fee may be less. The high ranked players like it because they play fewer matches before getting into the money.

Draw method -- Some random technique must be used to determine each person's initial position on the flow chart. When there are 16 or fewer players each player can draw a ball to determine their placement on the chart. When there are more than 16 players either position numbers or names can be drawn from a hat and entered on the chart in the order drawn.

Bye positions -- Two players are required to play a match and when there are an odd number of players in a frame, someone must get a *bye*. The player that is matched with the bye gets an automatic win and advances to the next frame.

When there are 2 players, or multiples thereof (4, 8, 16, etc.) no byes are required. When there are fewer players than there are chart positions, each vacant position must be filled with a bye. The byes must be uniformly distributed on the flow chart **before** player positions are selected.

Buy-in and buy-back -- There is another solution to the problem of having too many byes; it is called a *buy-in*. A buy-in means that an individual is allowed to enter the same tournament more than once and play in more than one position. A buy-in can be substituted for a bye thereby avoiding the injustice of giving someone an automatic win.

Probably the best way to treat vacant positions, on the single or double elimination chart, is by a combination of byes and buy-ins. This system is referred to as the *loser eligible buy-in* or *buy-back*. With this system the vacant positions are initially assigned byes, after each first frame match, the loser is given the option of buying back into the tournament at the last assigned bye position.

Flow chart -- The tournament flow chart should be large and visible to all the participants. This way all the participants can easily determine, for themselves, who they play next and where everyone is on the chart.

Scoring system -- The scoring system for single and double elimination tournaments is straightforward. The winner of the match advances on the flow chart and the loser doesn't. However, in a round robin tournament several different scoring systems can be used. It is imperative that the type of scoring system be specified before the tournament begins. Several types of scoring systems are examined in the book *THE SCIENCE OF POCKET BILLIARDS*.

Playing order -- There is no hard and fast rule as to the order in which the matches are played. Favoring the one loss side (playing first) in a double-elimination tournament will allow the losing players to go home as early as possible. Some tournament promoters (especially bars) want to keep everyone around for as long as possible so they play out the winner's bracket first. In any case, it is the tournament director's prerogative to determine who plays and when.

Playing order for a round robin tournament may have an affect on the final score. The players with the lowest number of wins should always play first. This accomplishes two things: First, the players that are most likely to win will play last; this keeps spectators interested to the very end. And second, the weaker player is less likely to concede games because the probability of losing the tournament is not evident in the early rounds.

Payout -- How the total prize fund is divided has a lot to do with the character of the tournament. If the top place is allocated a high amount, and only a few places are paid, the tournament will draw fewer but higher caliber players. If the prize fund is spread out among a large percentage (usually top 25 percent) of the players, more less-skilled players may participate.

Handicapping -- Everyone that enters a tournament hopes to have a chance at winning something. There is very little incentive for players with limited skill to enter a tournament if they have to play without a handicap against more skillful players. When there is a known disparity of playing skills, the weaker players may be given some sort of an advantage before the tournament begins; this is called handicapping. Handicapping helps to level the playing field and encourages players of all skill levels to participate in the same tournament.

There are many ways to handicap a player. In some tournaments the weaker player is given credit for one or more wins (commonly called "games on the wire") before the match begins. This means they don't have to win as many games as the better player in order to win the match.

Another form of handicapping is to give the weaker player an extra ball or balls (in addition to the 9-ball) to constitute a win. In normal play, making the 9-ball is the only way to win a game. If a player is given an extra ball, for example the 8-ball, that player

162

can win by making the 8- or 9-ball. Another technique is to let the weaker player "skip" a certain ball or balls.

A graduated entry fee is another way of handicapping a tournament. The better players pay a larger entry fee. This does not give the less skilled player a better chance of winning but it does increase the net payoff so that if they do win, they win more money.

Many NINE-BALL tournaments are restricted to players that are of a specific skill level. Ranking systems vary but the most common is the letter ranking system, which goes from **"A"** to **"D."** Players that are just below professional level are considered to be **"A"** players and **"D"** players are those that come in at the bottom in a barroom tournament.

You should find out in advance what kind of handicap system, if any, is being employed before signing up for a tournament.

♦ ♦ ♦

PERSONAL SCHEDULING

The longer a tournament takes the more you will have to plan ahead. You must make up your own schedule of personal activities such as eating, drinking, entertainment, resting, etc. Do <u>not</u> try to conduct your activities in accordance with someone else's schedule. If you are with friends, relatives, or other players, it is tempting to go along with the crowd. Resist that temptation. Every individual has his or her own wants, needs, and desires; yours must take precedent when you're playing in a tournament.

◆ ◆ ◆

FOOD AND REST

Food -- You must start controlling what you eat at least one day before the tournament begins. What you eat the day before will determine how your lower digestive tract will feel the day of the tournament. Don't experiment with new and different foods; eat only those foods that you are familiar with. Bland mundane foods are usually the best and safest.

When you eat a variety of foods at one sitting your stomach will secrete enough acid to digest the least digestible food. Therefore, the amount of acid in your stomach will be dictated by the most difficult to digest item of food. The rest of the food will have too much acid. The excess acid will only cause problems. Carry an antacid with you; use them at the first sign of acid distress.

It is always a good idea to carry your own water and snacks to the tournament room. Strange water, even though it may be excellent water, could cause a stomach problem for a short period. Don't eat any hard to digest food (like a hamburger) between games. If you get hungry, eat fruit or energy bars, which can be purchased at most grocery stores.

Note: The high-energy bars that are sold at most grocery stores make excellent snacks. Most have a long shelf life (six months to a year), don't need refrigeration, and are highly nutritious. There are many different types so try them all to find the one that best suits your needs.

Rest -- You cannot play your best pool unless you are well rested. Very often your sleep schedule, at the tournament, will be different from what you are use to. In these cases you may have to start adjusting your sleeping schedule several days prior to the tournament.

As your skill increases you will probably have to travel farther and farther from your home base to get to an appropriate tournament. You may eventually get far enough away from home that, to get the proper rest, you will have to stay in a motel. It may be difficult to sleep in a motel with strange sounds, surroundings, bed, etc. Your ability to sleep comfortably depends largely on your pillow. Some people find it best to travel with their own familiar pillow.

The biggest distraction to sustained sleep is noise. There are usually street noises, noises coming from the next room, ice machine noises, and conversations in the hall to name a few. The cheapest and simplest way to resolve a noise problem is to wear earplugs. Unfortunately, many people find earplugs to be uncomfortable when worn for a sustained period. Another way of resolving a noise problem is to train yourself to sleep with the noise of your choice (white noise, music, etc.). Your own familiar noise will drowned out the strange noises allowing you to sleep soundly.

It is best to room alone, or at least; don't room with anyone that you haven't roomed with before. They most likely won't have the same sleep schedule as yours; they may disturb your sleep by their restlessness; or, they may have bad habits like snoring. In short, if they have any problems they will become your problems.

Take along your own battery powered alarm clock. And remember, if you set a radio clock to a good radio station at night, the same station may not be on in the morning. Use a bell, tape, or CD alarm to wake you up (do not trust room service).

Even if you are not actually able to sleep well, lying quietly in bed is the next best thing. Quietly resting is not as good as actual sleep, but it does have some value. If you can't sleep at night, try taking a nap during the day. If all else fails, you may have to take a sleeping pill. Experiment before the tournament to find out what kind of sleeping pill works best for you. For many people a mild nighttime cough medicine works great. Be sure to follow the directions precisely. If it says not to take with alcohol, heed the warning. Even a slight numbing of the senses will adversely affect your pool game.

◆ ◆ ◆

RANDOM DRAW

When you draw a strong player don't think of it as bad luck, think of it as an opportunity to do something memorable. You won't remember defeating the unskilled players. But, if you beat the best player, you will have created an inspirational memory for all time. Beating the best player could likely be a bigger milestone in your pool career than winning the tournament. If you don't get a chance to play the best person you won't get a chance at that memory.

Another way of looking at drawing a tough player is that it takes all the pressure off of you. You have nothing to lose because you are not expected to win. Without the pressure you can play your best game.

If drawing the best player is so good, what if you draw the poorest player? Think of the poorest players as being stepping stones to the best player.

◆◆◆

OBSERVATIONS

Don't fritter away the time before and between matches. Observe ongoing games, check to see who is getting the best break and from what cue-ball position. Is the corner ball going in on the break? Is the 1-ball going into the side pocket? Is the 1-ball hitting before or after the side pocket? Is the cue-ball bouncing after impact with the 1-ball? Study the table roll; does the ball roll off on any part of the table? How forgiving are the pockets? How do the balls bank, long or short? Are the cushions dead or active? Is the table fast or slow? Knowing the answers to these questions will help you in getting a fast start. If your opponent waits untill the game to determine the answers, you will have an advantage.

Check out your opponents. Do they frustrate easily? What frustrates them? Do they like to play fast? Will a few good safeties disrupt their rhythm? What kind of shots do they prefer? Do they take the push-out option? Ask your friends what they know about your opponent.

◆ ◆ ◆

PRE-MATCH WARM UP

Before your pre-match warm up (immediately before the match begins) you should know how the table is playing from your observations. Your pre-match warm up should be used to get your mind and body in a game mode.

Start by stretching your neck and shoulder muscles. Muscle stretching before an event has been tested and proven to be beneficial in many other types of sports. So, it stands to reason that it is probably beneficial to the pool player as well.

The generally accepted format for warming up is for each player, in turn, to roll all nine balls on the table and shoot them in. It is acceptable to reposition a missed ball and shoot it again. However repeating that process too many times is considered bad manners. Generally, the players alternate shooting racks of balls until the match begins.

During your warm-up, it is advisable to shoot a few lag shots (as in lag for the break). This should be done even if the breaker is determined by a flip of a coin. Because the lag shot is strictly a speed control shot it will give you a good feel for the speed of the table. When you start the game, the weakest part of your game will probably be your speed control. As a match goes on, both players generally get better and better at their shape speed. If you practice the lag shot before the match begins, you will come out of the gate with a slight edge in speed control.

When you roll the balls onto the table (for your warm-up shots) be sure that there are no clusters or other difficult situations. You want all the shots to be easy. Keep in mind, you are only trying to loosen up and alert your muscles to the pending task, not challenge them to their limits. Try to make all your shots. Frequently, you may see a player miss a shot and set it up over and over only to miss it each time. Don't make that mistake. If you miss a shot, when you set it up for a second attempt make it a little easier than the first shot. If you continue to miss the shot, continue to make it easier until you do make it. Again, you are not challenging your skills, you are only trying to make balls and keep your confidence up.

If there is something unique about the equipment this is the time to get accustomed to it. Does the table roll off? Are the balls dirty and therefore throw more than you are use to? Are the pockets bigger or smaller

169

than you are use to? Try to adjust to these unique characteristics faster than your opponent. The worst thing you can do is dwell on table irregularities— accept them and resolve to adjust faster than your opponent. Pretend it is your idea to play on a flawed table because you know you can adjust faster than your opponent. Let your opponent spend the first half of the match complaining and the second half adjusting; by then you will have won.

Everyone's capabilities are a little different. You should know how many games it takes to get you in peak performance mode. If it only takes a few shots, there is no problem. If it takes several hours and many games you should find another table to shoot on before the pre-match warm up.

After you get warmed up, don't go off and do something else before starting the match. This only leads to cluttering of thoughts in the head and the task at hand becomes clouded with other thoughts.

It is normal to be tense before a match begins. However, some people get so tense that they get a headache. If you're one of them, come to the tournament prepared. Always carry aspirins in your cue case for these emergencies. If your stomach gets butterflies before a match, take an antacid. Monitor your body before and during a tournament. Any problems you have at one tournament may recur at other tournaments. Be prepared to treat the problems before they get a chance to affect your game.

♦ ♦ ♦

MENTAL CONSIDERATIONS

Tournament site -- If you are playing the tournament at a familiar site you have what is termed the "home field advantage." The home field advantage involves familiarity with the table as well as the total environmental setting. Your subconscious mind is distracted by all things that are unfamiliar. If you're playing at an unfamiliar site, there are things you should do to familiarize yourself with the surroundings. Before the tournament, study the venue in detail. What kind of artwork is on the walls? What color are the walls? Where are the toilets? Where is the bar? Where will the waitress be walking? Where are the entry and exit doors? What kind of food is on the menu? By becoming familiar with all these seemingly insignificant details your subconscious mind will no longer be distracted by them.

Tournament jitters -- Few people can play in an important tournament without getting emotional in some manner. Pre-game jitters may include fear, anxiety, butterflies, etc. With all these emotions running rampant, your body chemistry may even change. The change in chemistry may cause you to perspire, throw up, or respond in a number of other ways.

During play you may suffer from what is commonly known as choking. Choking is characterized by rapid heart rate, rapid shallow breathing, and general nervousness. You must know when to expect the emotional turmoil, what

171

conditions bring it on, and what the physical manifestations are. When you know what the problems are likely to be, it becomes easier to deal with them.

Mental barrier -- Some people have a psychological aversion to winning pool tournaments. They consistently get close (demonstrating that they have the talent) but never quite get the cigar. When these people finally manage to win, they usually become consistent winners. It's like there is a glass barrier between almost winning and winning. When this barrier is broken, winning becomes more achievable.

When people have a barrier problem, it is usually because winning is unfamiliar territory. It is more comfortable to be in familiar territory than in unfamiliar territory. The problem is finding a way to get that first win so you can become comfortable with winning.

The best way to break the barrier is to do it in your imagination. Try to visualize having won many times in the past. Imagine all the little details like offering condolences to the person you beat, accepting the congratulatory offerings and winnings. If you can accurately and convincingly imagine these images you will have broken the barrier.

Determination -- The person with the greatest determination has an advantage. Determination may not be the deciding factor but it will always be a contributing factor. There are two distinct types of determination, *immediate* and *long term*.

172

Immediate determination is what you are feeling at a particular time; when you're playing a game you have immediate determination. Immediate determination can best be measured in intensity rather than duration. Determination is needed at all times but is especially needed when you get behind in a match. If you get behind by a score of zero to five, in a race to seven, you may feel more discouraged than determined. But this is exactly the type of situation where determination will do the most good. Tell yourself; if your opponent can win five out of five games so can you. Remember, no matter how far behind you get, you only have to duplicate what your opponent did in order to get even; and, if your opponent can do it so can you.

Long-term determination is much more powerful than short-term determination. Long-term determination can best be measured in duration rather than intensity. Long-term determination will drive you to the practice table and keep you there. It will make you shoot the same shot over and over till you get it right. It will cause you to want to practice longer and harder than your opponent. If your opponent practiced bank shots for an hour you will practice them for two hours. If your opponent reads one instructional book you will read three. Without long-term determination, short-term determination is not effective.

Psyching by your opponent -- There will be times when your opponent will try to psych you out. There are many techniques that people use to psych out their opponents. To list these techniques would only draw attention to them and make matters worse.

If you think your opponent is doing something to deliberately distract you from your game, try to ignore it. Think of it as an act of desperation, your opponent obviously doesn't think he/she can win on skill alone. If you're the type of person that doesn't want to (or can't) ignore the psyching, plan your reaction in advance. Respectfully ask him/her to stop, (prepare your words in advance) if he/she doesn't comply, ask the tournament director to have a talk with him/her.

Sportsmanship -- Sportsmanship is largely a state of mind. It is important to demonstrate sportsmanship even when your opponent doesn't. People are watching, be presentable, your reputation (and possibly sponsorship) depends on your demeanor.

Be sensitive both as a winner and as a loser. If you win a match treat it with moderated enthusiasm. Remember, the loser of the match feels just as bad as you feel good. The emotional pain of losing a match is extremely intense immediately after the match but subsides quickly with time. Win or lose, a handshake and the exchange of a few words are generally considered good etiquette. Rehearse what you will say to the loser if you win or to the winner if you lose. Having a rehearsed response is safer than having to be spontaneous at these highly emotional times.

◆ ◆ ◆

PLAYING THE MATCH

Stay informed -- Should you keep track of the flow chart? Some people don't like to know, in advance, whom they will be playing but it is usually better to have this information. Knowing who your opponent is will help avoid last minute surprises—surprises are never beneficial. Knowing whom you are playing allows you to better plan your strategy and visualize winning.

Early game -- If all the emotion is taken out of the analysis, the first shot of the first game is just as important as the last shot in a hill-hill game. Actually, the first few shots are even more important than the last few shots because they set the pace for the entire match. If you make that first shot the tension is broken, your opponent is disappointed and the tone is set.

Guard against taking a less skilled player lightly. The shorter the race, the easier it is for the weaker player to steal a game (or a match). There are ways of avoiding this: When shooting a less skilled player don't simply try to win, you should resolve to win by X games. When you set a higher performance standard you are less likely to be lethargic when playing the first few games.

Risk-reward -- Each shot has a component of *risk* and a potential for *reward*. Risk is a subjective determination of probable success and consequence of failure. Reward is the positive result of a properly executed shot. An accurate evaluation of both must be made when assessing a potential shot. If both are not kept in balance your game will suffer.

In a tournament there usually are spectators observing the action. When being observed there is a tendency for a competitor to take more risks than usual (show off). Psychologist have a term for this tendency, it's called *risky shift*. Risky shift is motivated by a desire to please the spectators. Consistency and caution generally are not as crowd pleasing as spectacular flamboyance. Fight the tendency to show off.

Keeping score -- In the absence of a more elaborate scoring system, the number of games won can be recorded using a coin. A coin for each player is placed under the cushion at the center diamond at the head of the table. The player's coin is moved one diamond for each win (pockets don't count) away from each other. The easy way to count total games won is to remember that the head cushion has just one move (diamond) and all succeeding rails represent three wins between pockets.

Always use a specific routine when you win a game. For example, immediately on winning a game collect all balls from the head and side pockets and roll them to the foot of the table. Then, mark your score before you sit down or do anything else. When you use a specific routine there is less chance of not recording your score or recording it twice.

◆ ◆ ◆

POST TOURNAMENT ANALYSIS

A lot can be learned by looking back and analyzing your tournament performance. But be very careful about evaluating each aspect of your game. The score does not always reflect the level of one's play. You may pocket more balls (play better) than your opponent and still lose the game. Whether you win or lose is usually a result of a complicated interaction of both players. Who is responsible when a batter hits a home run, the batter or the pitcher? Was it superior play by the batter or inferior play by the pitcher?

Keeping a tournament diary can be beneficial. When the tournament is over write down your thoughts and observations. Try to analyze why various things happened. The following are some of the topics that should be addressed:

Eating: Did anything you ate cause a problem? Is there anything you ate that you recommend for the next tournament? Should you have eaten more or less than you did? Was drinking a problem?

Sleep: Did you get adequate rest? Was your sleep scheduling good or bad? Any suggestions for the next tournament?

Players: Are there any unique characteristics that you should remember about any of the other players? Who did you play and what was the score?

Activities: In what kind of outside activities did you participate? Did any of your activities have an influence on your pool playing?

Associations: Are there any people or players you should associate with, or avoid, in the future? Did your friends do anything to influence your game? Any future advice for your friends?

Shots: Were there any shots that you should practice more or examine more closely? What kind of shots do you need to concentrate on in practice?

Equipment: Did all your equipment function well? Do you need a new tip on your stick? Was the chalk adequate? Do you need a jump stick? Was there anything unique about the table that you liked or disliked?

◆ ◆ ◆

SPECTATING

Even though you are a participant in a tournament you won't be actively playing all the time—at times you will be a spectator. And, as a spectator you have a responsibility to avoid disturbing the people that are playing.

When you're sitting in the front row, or anywhere near the active tables, you are obligated to know what is going on at all times. You must not move when a player is shooting in your direction, don't applaud when a player is about to shoot etc. If you're paying attention to the game directly in front of you, your spontaneous reactions are generally not a problem. However, a problem can result if you're watching a match that is not on the nearest table. You may clap or otherwise react to something that is happening on an adjacent table. In so doing you may disrupt the players on the near table.

If you talk with your hands or are hard-of-hearing, don't sit in the front row. If you have any nervous twitches like shaking your foot or tapping your fingers, don't sit in the front row. Keep in mind, you must make allowances for those players that are much more sensitive about disturbances than you are. You are expected to conform to their disturbance standards not yours.

You must take personal responsibility for the behavior of the friends you bring to the tournament. In their enthusiasm they may be tempted to yell and scream to cheer you on. That kind of behavior is very disruptive to all the players. What is even worse is applauding when your opponent does something wrong. That type of behavior is totally unacceptable.

It is important that your friends don't disturb your opponent; it is just as important that they don't unknowingly disturb you. If you are going to associate with friends be sure to give them some instruction on how to behave while around you. No complaining, no negative comments, no problems to solve, no unsolicited advice or analysis, no questions, etc.

♦♦♦

SPONSORSHIP

One of the things that helps keep professional sports running is sponsorship money. Events are sponsored and players are sponsored. Without sponsorship money most professional sports would fail.

Events -- Everyone knows that big time sporting events have big time corporate sponsorship. They pay for signage, advertisements in programs, equipment, prize money, and many other things. This type of sponsorship system does not have to be confined to big events. The same motivational forces exist regardless of the size of the event. Even small barroom tournaments should seek out sponsorship even though it may be on a smaller scale.

Players -- Not everybody can be a world class professional but most players can be at the top of some smaller venue. That is, you could be the top player in your company, your block, your zip code etc. Even if you are nowhere near pro level, you can still solicit sponsorship. Solicit the local taverns, billiard supply stores, grocery stores, or any other businesses in the area. Sponsorship does not have to be based on a long formal contract when you are operating at the lower levels. For example, you could wear a sponsor's shirt in return for all or part of your entry fee. Be sure to insist that the tournament director announces your sponsor's name when referring to you (this may influence other potential sponsors to participate). Don't be embarrassed by starting small, the better you get the more attractive you will be to the sponsors. By starting early and small you will be getting good experience as well as exposure. As your skills progress and you enter bigger and bigger tournaments, you can become more selective about whose products you endorse.

If you dress well, speak well, and act well, you should be able to get sponsorship at some level. Sponsors don't like to take a chance, if they think there is a chance that you will do something embarrassing, they cannot, and will not, take a chance on you. No sponsor wants to be represented by someone that may get caught taking dope or doing some other dumb thing. When you play you are a reflection of your sponsor, if you embarrass yourself, you embarrass your sponsor.

You may even play better if you are sponsored. Look around; if you are the only person that is being sponsored, you have a psychological edge.

◆ ◆ ◆